New Beginnings

Things to Know to Become a Better Christian

New Beginnings

Things to Know to
Become a Better Christian

by Don Dilmore

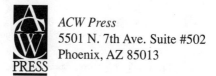

ACW Press
5501 N. 7th Ave. Suite #502
Phoenix, AZ 85013

Cover design by Eric Walljasper
Page design by Prelude to Print

Unless otherwise noted, all Scripture quotations are from The Holy Bible, New International Version, copyright © 1973, 1978, 1984 International Bible Society. Used by permission of Zondervan Bible Publishers.

I am grateful to Campus Crusade for Christ for allowing me to quote the **Four Spiritual Laws** in this book. Copyrighted 1965,1994 by Bill Bright, New Life Publications, Campus Crusade for Christ. All rights reserved. Used by permission.

Publisher's Cataloging-in-Publication
(Provided by Quality Books, Inc.)

Dilmore, Don
    New beginnings: things to know to become a
better Christian/ by Don Dilmore — 1st ed.
    p. cm.
    Includes bibliographical references.
    ISBN 1-89252-518-6

    1. Christian Life—Southern Baptist authors.
    2. Southern Baptist Convention—Doctrines.
    I. Title

BV4501.2.D55 1999   248.4'86132
                       QBI99-1137

This book is dedicated to Marie, my faithful wife of over forty-nine years, who has been a wonderful and loving mother to our children. Thank you for standing by me through thick and thin, and for always being faithful to our Lord and Savior, Jesus Christ

Acknowledgements

My deepest thanks to Dr. Richard Blackaby, President of the Canadian Southern Baptist Seminary, Cochrane, Alberta; Dr. Pete Freeman, pastor of the First Baptist Church, The Woodlands, Texas; and Dr. Donn Taylor, author, The Woodlands, Texas. They all assisted me greatly with their ideas and suggestions and proofreading of the text.

Thanks also to Steve Laube and his staff at ACW Press for exercising their skills in publishing this book.

Introduction

This book is directed toward new Christians as well as those who feel they have been lacking in their commitment to God. It was written in the hope that the reader will grow and mature into a Spirit-filled Christian. My purpose is to help those who are new in the faith, as well as those who want to grow spiritually, to gain a better grasp of what it truly means to be a Christian, whether they are ten or seventy. It is my prayer that you will grasp a better appreciation of your heritage if you are a Southern Baptist.

If you are embarking on the journey as a new Christian, I pray that it will be a New Beginning in the fullest sense of the word. I know some Christians are disappointed because they had hoped their life would be different after they accepted Christ. In truth, it has been no different for many because they did nothing to grow in the grace bestowed upon them.

God can help us change our lives so that we put the emphasis in the right place and find our complete joy in the things of God. But He can't change us unless we are willing to be changed and then work diligently to help make that change come about.

You will find yourself well on the way to a New Beginning in the Lord Jesus Christ if you will do the following: (1) faithfully, over the next thirteen weeks, study one chapter a week, (2) look up the scriptures where it is required, (3) complete the daily work assignment, and (4) put into practice what you have learned.

This is not a theological treatise. This is a book for laypeople who are new in Christ, written by a layman who has known Him for sixty-two years and is still learning.

Foreword

by Dr. Richard Blackaby,
President Canadian Southern Baptist Seminary

Don and Marie Dilmore have been a blessing to every church they have been a part of. They both have a heart for God, and love to encourage others to follow God, as they have done so faithfully themselves.

Don has been a teacher for over forty-three years, helping people to grow deeper in their walk with God. This book is a summary of the wide teaching he has been providing new Christians. You will find that it will bless you as it has blessed many others over the years. God wants our lives to be changed as we follow HIM. This book will provide you with guidelines to make those changes.

Instructions

You should be able to complete this book in thirteen weeks. Hopefully you will have a mentor assigned to you for this period of time. You may also have a class meeting once a week to discuss the previous week's lesson. If you study without someone to mentor or teach you should follow the same schedule.

You need to read a chapter each week. You may choose to read the entire chapter at one time, or to split it up and read a few pages each day. If you read the entire chapter at one time, please read it early in the week, perhaps Sunday afternoon or Monday evening.

Then each day, starting after the last chapter you will find a daily assignment. Most, but not all of these will include looking up some scripture, answering a couple of questions regarding what you have read, and each day an item to pray about. The idea, quite frankly, is to get you into the habit of studying your Bible and praying every day.

You will also find assignments to memorize the books of the Bible, to enable you to find Scripture readily. Please do this. You will never be sorry. It is a great advantage to be able to locate passages of scripture easily.

If you are meeting in a class of new Christians, be sure you join a Sunday School class the week you finish this book. If you are not meeting with a new Christian group, join a Sunday School class this next Sunday.

Contents

CHAPTER 1

Am I Really Saved?

*I*sn't it exciting to be a new Christian? Doesn't it make you feel good to know the Bible says you are a "joint heir" with Jesus? That means that you are inheriting all that belongs to the Son of God. Some new Christians find this hard to believe. They ask questions, such as, "Am I really saved?" "Am I really going to heaven?" "Am I really one of God's children?" The answer is yes you are saved, and you are now one of His children if you have committed your life to Him. Those are some of the issues we will discuss in this book.

I know you want to get the most out of being a Christian. You now want to please God with the way you live your life. You may just need to have some questions answered. You may be reading this while you are still wrestling with a decision to follow Christ. If so, you could be saying: "Is this all there is to being a Christian? There must be more to it. There must be something else I have to do." Or, "I'm too bad to be saved. Does God really love *me*?"

You may even have several questions you have been embarrassed to ask. Doubts may have come up in the back of your mind. The purpose of this book is to provide more information to new Christians and prospective Christians. So let's start by looking at salvation, the commitment from God about the rest of eternity.

First of all, God expects us to accept Him by faith. You may say, "That is a lot to ask. Why should I take someone by faith I have never seen. How can I trust my eternal destiny to someone I have never met."

Have you ever worked in or gone to see someone in a very tall building forty, sixty, or eighty stories high? Did you take the elevator? Most of us have had that experience at least once. If you live in a large city, you may do it every day. Did you meet the people who installed the elevators? Do you know their names? Did you check out their training credentials? Did you go to the company where the elevators were made to ensure that they were made with the best materials?

Did you go down in the basement of the building and crawl in the elevator shaft or climb the stairs to the roof to check out the steel cables before you rode the first time? Do you know the people who maintain the elevators? Are they trustworthy and competent? I doubt you could answer very many of these questions in the affirmative. If you are like most of us, you walk into the elevator, push the button for the floor you want to visit, and you expect the door will close and the elevator will take you safely to your floor. We take the elevator by *faith*. You have faith in those who built it, installed it, and maintain it. Though you've never seen them, or know them, you have faith in them. You and hundreds of others who ride those elevators expect them to perform safely.

You do things by faith many times every day without even thinking about it. You have faith that the other driver is going to stop at the red light. You have faith that the mailman will bring your mail without taking out what he wants first. You have faith that your boss will give you a paycheck when the week's work is over. All day long, you practice faith as you go about your tasks, sometimes with people you never see.

You see and talk to your boss and the mailman every day, or at least fairly frequently. Others, you may never cross paths with, like the elevator maintenance man. But if you stop to think about it, it should be much easier to have faith in God. He created this whole universe. He was here before time began. Everything goes according to His plan. It should not be difficult to accept by faith that He loves you and will provide for you IF YOU TRUST IN HIM.

The Bible tells us that we need to "live by faith." To be more specific, 1 Corinthians16:13 says, "Be on your guard; stand firm in the faith; be men of courage, be strong." And 2 Corinthians 5:7 tells us, "We live by faith, not by sight." It is important that we have faith in God, that we trust Him for all things.

This brings us back to the question about being saved. Some who read this book may have become Christians several weeks or months ago. Others may have made a profession of faith very recently. There are probably some who read this who have not yet taken that step. Because a commitment to follow Christ is the most important thing you will ever do, I want to be sure that you understand how you become a Christian.

There are several ways that are used to explain to a person "how to be saved." Some people use Scriptures out of the book of Romans in the Bible. This is called the Roman Road to Salvation. Others may use Scriptures from several books of the Bible. Dr. Bill Bright, who founded Campus Crusade for Christ, developed a booklet called "Four Spiritual Laws." These laws are backed up by Scriptures to explain them. It is a simple way to understand "how to be saved." Let's look at those four laws.

Law One: "God loves you and offers you a wonderful plan for your life." He uses a Scripture you may have heard several times to explain this. "God so loved the world that He gave His one and only Son, that whoever believes in Him shall not perish but have eternal life" (John 3:16) God loves all of us and wants the best for us, but why is it that many people are not experiencing the kind of life God desires for them? That is covered in the next law.

Law Two: "Man is sinful and separated from God. Therefore he cannot know and experience God's love and plan for his life." Romans 3:23 says, "All have sinned and fall short of the glory of God." God wants the best for us, but He gives us the right and the freedom to choose. Some people choose separation from God by their actions, living their lives in ways that are not pleasing to God. Others may live fairly decent lives but are indifferent to God, ignoring Him and His wishes for them. In either case, they are separated from God. That separation is like a deep canyon or a great gulf that separates man from God. Men try to reach up to God by studying philosophy, or just being good, but that doesn't restore the broken relationship. Which brings us to:

Law Three: "Jesus Christ is God's _only_ provision for man's sin. Through Him you can know and experience God's love and plan for your life." Romans 5:8 tells us that "God demonstrates His own love toward us, in that while we were yet sinners, Christ died for us." In John 14:6 Jesus said, "I am the way, and the truth, and the life, no one comes to the Father but through Me." So God spanned the gulf that separates men from God by sending His Son to die on the cross for our sins. That is God's grace. _Grace_ is a word you will bump into quite often as a Christian. It means "kindness towards mankind shown by the Lord Jesus."[1] He died on the cross for our sins because He loves us with an unfathomable love. But we need to understand:

Law Four: "We must individually receive Jesus Christ as Savior and Lord; then we can know and experience God's love and plan for our lives." John 1:12 says, "As many as received

Him, to them He gave the right to become children of God, even to those who believe in His name."[2] Ephesians 2:8-9 tells us, "By grace you have been saved through faith, and that not of yourselves, it is the gift of God; not as a result of works that no one should boast." God saved us by His grace. We accept that salvation by believing in Him, by having faith in Him, and in repentance, which is the changing of our life style. We will talk more about repentance in chapter 5. We will talk a lot more about changing our lives throughout this book. But at this point, you should understand that no matter how bad you may have been in the past, or how indifferent to God you have been, you are now saved if you believe that God sent His Son to die on the cross for your sins and then was resurrected from the dead. If you believe this and repent, you have been saved. You can put away the questions and doubts. God's Word is true, and He has declared that His grace has saved you.

You may not be a Bible scholar, but let me direct you to some Scriptures that show what God has done for others and how He changed their lives. These verses will give you a better idea of how your life will be changed if you put your faith and trust in God.

It is a known fact that as most people get older, they get more and more set in their ways. It is hard to get adults to change their habits. They have a fixed routine, with certain things they like and dislike, and it takes a lot for them to try something new or to change their ways. I want to cite two examples of men who came to know Jesus and how their lives were changed as they truly realized who He was. They had to have believed in Him for their lives to have changed so dramatically overnight.

We are going to start using our Bible here. If you don't have a Bible, now is the time to buy one. We will try to give you some helpful hints in chapter 3 about what kind of Bible to buy. If you cannot afford one, ask a Christian friend or someone in your church office to help you. I am sure they will find one for you to use.

We want to look in the New Testament, in the book of Matthew. If you don't know where it is, look in the front of your Bible in the Table of Contents, where you will find the page number. We will go into more detail later on how to learn where to find things in your Bible, but for now turn to Matthew. It is the first book in the New Testament section of your Bible. You will find each book in the Bible divided into chapters, and we want to find chapter 26.

Prior to the time we are reading about, Jesus had been arrested. It is just before His crucifixion, and He is appearing before the High Priest in a hearing. Peter, one of Jesus' disciples, has followed and is in the courtyard outside. Now read verses 69-75 in Matthew 26.

Here we have a picture of one of the men who had been with Jesus as a devout disciple. He had heard Him preach. He had seen Him heal people. He had been an almost constant companion for Jesus' three years of ministry. Now, when he is put to the test, Peter fails miserably. When questioned by a girl in the courtyard, he is afraid for his life. The Bible tells us he even curses as he denies that he is one of Jesus' followers, or that he even knows Him.

Now turn over four books. Go past Mark, Luke, John and stop in Acts. Be sure you do this as we go along. I want you to get used to looking up things in your Bible. Start reading in Acts 2:1 and read the whole second chapter. Read it carefully. I'll wait for you.

What does it tell us? Yes! That is the same Peter. The man who was so scared he denied even knowing Jesus just a few weeks ago now stands in front of thousands of people and pleads with them to follow Jesus. We talked earlier about the fact that adults don't change easily. To see what changed Peter, we need to go back to the book of Luke, the third book in the New Testament. Remember, we just passed by there between

Matthew and Acts. Read Luke 24:13 and continue to the end of the chapter. That is what changed Peter. He had an encounter with the resurrected Jesus. He had seen Jesus crucified. He knew His body had been placed in a tomb. And now he sees Him alive again. He had witnessed the power and love of God at its very best. God sent His Son to die on the cross and to be resurrected that our sins might be forgiven so that we might have eternal life. It is hard to not believe something when you have an eyewitness whose life has been transformed by what he has seen.

The second story we are going to read begins in Acts, chapter 7. This chapter contains a sermon preached by a young Christian man named Stephen. Read his sermon carefully and then pay particular attention to another young man named Saul. His name appears in verse 58, and then again in chapter 8, verses 1 and 3.

Let's look at Saul for a minute. Here we find a man who was zealously seeking out Christians to persecute them. He was a devout and highly educated Jew. He had been trained to believe that the Messiah would come to save the Jewish people. He believed that this Messiah would be a mighty warrior who would free the Jews from Roman rule and lead them to a place of prominence in the world. Jesus' followers said that He was the Messiah. Saul and the other religious leaders asked, "How could this Jesus be the Messiah, when he is just the son of a carpenter, with a few fishermen and other uneducated people as his followers?" To Saul, this was heresy. So Saul took it upon himself to track down these followers of Jesus and have them killed. We don't have to go far to see that God changed this man's life in an amazing way. Read chapter 9, verses 1-31 in the book of Acts.

Did God change Saul's life? Yes! He changed him dramatically from a killer of Christians into a faithful believer and the first missionary. He even changed his name from Saul to Paul. Paul went out into all parts of the known world and preached about Jesus. He started churches and trained men to be the pastors of those churches that sprung up because of his missionary work. He wrote letters of encouragement back to them. We will see later that a good part of the New Testament is made up of those letters, which are called epistles.

I want to call your attention to the fact that these two men, Peter and Paul, were amazingly transformed because they had an encounter with God. They were no longer the same. They serve not only as proof that there is a God and that he loves us, but also as a powerful example to us that our lives are to be changed when we become followers of Jesus. We are no longer the same. If we are serious about following Jesus, our friends and family will see a dramatic change in us.

Yes, God can change us. I also want you to remember that God is near you and that He really does love you. How do I know? I don't have space to share all the ways I know. Let me tell you one story that proved to me and to others that there is a God, and that He loves us with an ever-lasting love.

In 1962 my wife and I sat in the office of the chief neuro-surgeon at Southwestern Medical School in Dallas. We had been to five doctors that week with our four-year-old daughter Helen, the youngest of four children. The doctor said, "I understand that tomorrow Helen will be five years old." I nodded yes. He said, "Take her home and give her the biggest birthday party you can afford, because she won't be here for a sixth birthday. She has cancer in her sinus passage. It is a carcinoma. It is inoperable."

We were stunned, but we did what he had suggested. It was the most difficult birthday party I ever went through. For the next three years, we took her to radiation treatments and chemotherapy. Our lives were in and out of the hospital, not knowing from one day to the next what lay ahead. We sadly watched our daughter's frail body steadily decline and weaken. She got to the point of taking codeine every half hour for the pain. The doctors could no longer help her, so we kept her at home. She went into a coma. For five days and nights she had nothing to eat or drink and no medication. She didn't utter a single word. Her eyes were closed. On the fifth afternoon, the neurosurgeon, the chemotherapist, the pediatrician, and the opthamologist all came to our home. Each of them told us she couldn't live through the night. I went to the funeral home and made arrangements for the funeral.

When I arrived home, I told my wife I had made the arrangements. She said, "You didn't need to do that. Helen is going to get well. I have been praying that God would hear us and that He would heal her, and I have a calmness I have not had in a long time. God is going to answer our prayers. Helen is going to get well."

The next morning, we placed Helen on the couch, as we had for many mornings. About ten o'clock, she opened her eyes and said, "Daddy, I want a milkshake." And from that moment on, she started to get well.

Helen is now forty-two years old. She works full time as a Christian counselor, and she has a daughter, which is a miracle in itself, considering all of the chemotherapy and radiation her body had absorbed.

Was this a coincidence? An act of fate? The doctors don't think so. Early in Helen's illness we told one doctor that we wanted to pray about a procedure he wanted to perform on her. He laughed at us. "You don't really believe in God, do you?" he questioned. He is now a Christian. I heard him tell a nurse a few years after Helen's miraculous recovery, "No doctor or medicine healed that girl. God did that."

Why doesn't God heal all children whose parents pray? We'll talk more about that later, but we must believe that God is infinitely wiser than we will ever be, and He has a sovereign reason for everything that He does.

Suffice it to say, I saw God heal a little girl. And my wife and I felt His love throughout the experience, even during the times when we thought she was going to die. I have seen Him act over and over again. Jobs came in the height of despair and hopelessness; homes sold that enabled people to do what God wanted them to do; a seminary was built in a country where there was no Southern Baptist seminary, built by volunteer labor, and a large part of it was paid for by people 2,500 miles away. I also know of inoperable cancers that showed on the X-ray and weren't there when exploratory surgery was done.

God's work continues twenty-four hours a day around this world, and time after time you see His hand in the middle of it. Yes, there is a God, and He loves each of us. John 3:16 says, "For God so loved the world that He gave His one and only Son that whoever believes in Him shall not perish but have eternal life."

God loves you, and He sent His son to die on the cross so that the things you have done wrong in your life could be forgiven. You don't have to be a "bad person" to be a sinner. We have all done something that we need to be forgiven for, even if it was no more than ignoring God up to this point in our lives. Yet no matter how "good" or "bad" you have been, God is willing to forgive you. The only sin that is unforgivable is the sin of not believing in God and the gift of His Son.

It is God's will that we have the assurance of our salvation. Acts 2:21 says, "Everyone who calls on the name of the Lord will be saved." Read this carefully. It doesn't say that if we believe there is a God we will be saved. It says that if we call on the name of the Lord—if we trust in Him, if we believe in Him, if we truly understand that God sent His Son, born of the virgin Mary, to live on this earth, and that He died on the cross, and then was resurrected so that our sins could be forgiven—that belief coupled with God's grace is what saves us.

Now that we are saved, God's gift to us is eternal life. Open your Bible again to the fourth book in the New Testament, the book of John, and look in the fifth chapter. The twenty-fourth verse is part of a discussion Jesus is having with some Jewish leaders. He says, "I tell you the truth, whoever hears my word and believes Him who sent me, has eternal life and will not be condemned; he has crossed over from death to life." What does this mean? Jesus is saying that if we believe in Him, if we trust in God, we will not go to hell but will have an eternal life in heaven. When our physical body gives out, whether we are young or old, we will take our place in heaven. We will live forever in a kingdom prepared by our Heavenly Father. This is our promise.

A little further along in the Bible, Paul wrote in his letter to the Philippians, "But our citizenship is in heaven. And we eagerly await a Savior from there, the Lord Jesus Christ, who, by the power that enables Him to bring everything under His control, will transform our lowly bodies so that they will be like His glorious body." That Scripture is found in Philippians 3:20-21. (That is the way you will find Scripture references designated. The name of the book, then the chapter number and, after the colon, the verses.)

Paul says Christ is going to come again, and He will change our earthly bodies into heavenly, "glorious" bodies. We will no longer hurt, have aches and pains, but our body will be like Christ's resurrected body. I don't want to load too much on you at one time, but there will come a time when this heaven and earth will pass away, and God will create a new heaven and a new earth where we will live forever. What a promise! What a tremendous thing to look forward to. And what a motivation and encouragement to us to help our friends and family come to know Him.

To summarize: God has told us that if we believe that He sent His son, Jesus Christ, to live on this earth, to die on the cross, to be resurrected and return to heaven, and that if we repent, or change our ways, our sins will be forgiven, and we will have everlasting life with Him. Someday we will be going from our life here to a life with Him where there will be no more sorrow or pain.

I ask you, do you really trust Him? Do you really believe in Him? If so, you have gained a new freedom from doubts and fears. You are ready to start enjoying your life with Him, to have a new beginning. What you do with it is up to you. He will not coerce you. You have the freedom to make your own decisions. If you are sincere about following Him, and you want to receive the full benefit of being one of His children, then your life will be different than it has been in the past. You will seek His leadership in making all your decisions. There is nothing—big or small—that he is not concerned about. You will try your best to serve Him in all that you do. Your life will be changed. In the next several chapters we will look at how that change will take place.

I hope you are sincere in wanting to make your life different for Him. It's up to you. Reading the remainder of this book can help you get started. I encourage you to read on with a resolve to be all that He wants you to be.

One of my favorite stories is about a man who worked until midnight several nights a week. To get home from work, he rode the bus to the end of the line and then had to walk several blocks to reach his house. He found he could cut through the cemetery and get home much quicker. Others followed the same path, and someone had conveniently cut the fence to enable them to take the shortcut. One dark, rainy night as our friend got off the bus, he pulled his coat collar up tight around his neck, pulled his cap down over his forehead, and started a brisk walk home. When he got to the cemetery, he ducked through the hole in the fence and started across the well-worn path. He did not know that on that particular day they had opened a new gravesite directly in the path.

With his head down to avoid the rain, he didn't see the hole and he fell in. The sides of the hole were wet, muddy, and slippery, and try as he could, he couldn't get out. He knew he would have to wait until morning when the workers arrived, so he huddled down in the most sheltered corner of the grave and eventually fell asleep.

A few hours later, another man on his way home used the same pathway with the same result. He was frightened when he fell in and started yelling, Help me! Help me! Someone get me out of here!" The first man awoke, his voice now scratchy and gravelly from the cold and moisture. "You ain't gonna get out of here tonight," he said in a very raspy voice. But the second man did. And do you know why he did? Because he wanted to badly enough.

How much do you want to be all that God wants you to be? Do you want it with all your heart? Do you desire to be like Him enough to do exactly what He tells you to do? As you read the next few chapters, pay close attention to how He will help you mature into the person He wants you to be.

Endnotes

1 *Smith's Bible Dictionary* (A.J. Holman Co.)

2 *Four Spiritual Laws* (Campus Crusade for Christ, 1965)

CHAPTER 2

Who the Holy Spirit Is and What He Does

God, Jesus, Holy Spirit, Savior, Comforter, Creator, Heavenly Father—these are just a few of the names used for God in the Bible. Most of these names describe one of God's characteristics, or something of what He does. With all the names, it is still difficult for us to comprehend all that God is. He is so much more than we can envision because all we have to measure Him by is other people. God is much more than a person. He is not "The man upstairs," "The Sky Pilot," or some of the other slang expressions you may hear from those who don't understand who God really is. Don't get in the habit of addressing God irreverently. He deserves our greatest respect and awe because of who He is.

God is the Creator of everything. He created the universe. He is the most powerful being in the universe. Look in your Bible at Genesis 1:1. Remember, it is the first book in your Bible. That first verse tells us that God created everything. Now read the rest of the first chapter. Go ahead. I'll wait.

Now do you realize why we should not be flippant when we mention God? He is our Creator, and the Creator of all we see and have around us. He is all-powerful.

Realizing that God is all-powerful, with the ability to create the world around us, our oceans, mountains, and even life itself, then we shouldn't doubt His ability to do the things He has said He will do.

Probably the most difficult thing for a new Christian to grasp is that God makes himself known to us in three different ways: God the Father, Jesus the Son, and the Holy Spirit. You may have already sung the Hymn, *"Holy, Holy, Holy."* The last line says, "God in three persons, blessed Trinity." That is referring to the three forms that God takes. The word "trinity" means "a threefold personality," or "the state of being three." It is a word commonly used to refer to God the Father, God the Son, and God the Holy Spirit.

Perhaps the easiest way to explain this is to compare the "Trinity" with H_2O. When we say H_2O, we usually think of water that we drink or bathe in. But H_2O also takes on the form of ice when it is cold, and steam when it is very hot. All three are used for different purposes, but all three are H_2O.

God is our Heavenly Father. He is Jesus Christ the Son. He is the Holy Spirit, or the Comforter. He is just one person, but the same abilities that gave Him power to create the world also give Him the power to manifest himself in three different personalities. When He spoke as God to Moses in the desert, He was God the Father. (See Exodus 19:3.) When He needed a sacrifice for our sins, He took on the appearance of Jesus Christ the Son. When we became Christians, He put in us the third part of the Trinity—the Holy Spirit. For us, an impossibility; but for the Creator, all in a day's work. God the Father, God the Son, and God the Holy Spirit all perform different functions just as ice, water, and steam perform different functions.

In this chapter we want to talk about the function of the Holy Spirit. Why does God take this form, and what does He do as the Holy Spirit?

God has used the form of the Holy Spirit since the beginning of time. Psalm 104:30 tells us, "When you send your Spirit, they are created." In other words, the breath of every living thing depends on God's Spirit. In Job 33:4, Job says, "The Spirit of God has made me, the breath of the Almighty gives me life." So we see the work of the Holy Spirit in creation.

There are several instances in the Old Testament in which God used the form of the Holy Spirit to accomplish what He needed done. Numbers 27:18 says, "So the Lord said to Moses, 'Take Joshua son of Nun, a man in whom is the spirit.'" (Be sure to stop and look up these references as we go along.) Joshua was to become a leader of the Israelites, and God put the Holy Spirit in him that he might become a great leader. Of course, he could have refused to heed the Spirit in his life and been a failure in doing God's work. But he was filled with the Spirit so that he might have the opportunity to lead God's people.

Read Daniel 5:11-14. Here again we see God using the Holy Spirit to guide one of His chosen ones. As you come back and read the entire book of Daniel in the next few months, you will discover why God used the Spirit to bless Daniel's work in the Babylonian empire.

In chapter 6 we will talk about reading through the Bible. As you do this, you will better understand why God uses the form of the Holy Spirit in many situations to accomplish His work.

Look at Exodus 31:1-5. Here God used His Spirit to give a man special skills to help in building the Ark of the Covenant, the place where the Ten Commandments were to be kept.

Judges 14:6 tells of "the Spirit of the Lord" coming upon Samson "in power, so that he tore the lion apart."

I hope you are beginning to grasp the significance of God in the form of the Holy Spirit. He provides leadership, mental powers, physical skills, strength for protection. But take careful note: God uses the form of the Holy Spirit only to accomplish His will. The Spirit was never used only for the purpose of a person's personal gain.

Let's look at some other ways God has used the Holy Spirit to accomplish His work.

First, God used the Holy Spirit in the writing of the Bible. Second Timothy 3:16 tells us that Scripture is God-breathed. We will talk about this in chapter 3. The Spirit was the inspiration that put the words into the minds of God's servants who penned these documents we know as The Holy Bible. There are three words that we need to look at here. **Revelation** relates to the content or material in the Bible. **Inspiration** pertains to the method of recording the material. And **Illumination** refers to the meaning. The Holy Spirit is the One who reveals, inspires, and illumines.

The second thing we need to realize about the Ministry of the Holy Spirit is how He participates in the salvation (saving) of people. God wants us to be saved. He loves all people no matter their color, race, sex, or education. None of these makes a difference to Him. John 3:16 says, "God so loved the *world*"—not just some of the people in the world. He loves **all** of us. He wants all of us to be Christians, but He leaves the decision to us. Read John 16:7-11.

Here Jesus is telling His followers that He is going back to heaven. When He does, the Counselor (Holy Spirit) will come, and one of His jobs will be to "convict" (set forth the truth of the Gospel) so people will be aware of their sins and of God's forgiveness if they trust in Him. The Spirit speaks through preachers, evangelists, and laypeople who make themselves available to Him for that purpose. Then it is up to each person to make his or her decision.

I read recently about a young lady in Communist Russia who told of her life thirty years ago when no missionaries or Bibles were allowed in the country. Yet the Holy Spirit, working through other books, made her aware of God's love, and she became a Christian without any direct contact with another Christian person.

The Holy Spirit uses people like our missionaries, scattered all across the world, to spread His Word despite language and cultural barriers.

God also uses the Holy Spirit to lead people to Him in your hometown. Let me cite an example. For many years I have been actively involved in church visitation. I get cards from the church with names of people who have visited the church or people someone in the church has suggested we visit. I also pray frequently that God will bring people across my path who want to know how to become Christians. A few years ago, I was out on a cold, dark winter night making some of those visits. I had made three calls and found no one at home. I was cold and a little discouraged, so I decided to call it quits and go home to watch Monday night football.

I started driving across town toward our home, but the Holy Spirit had a different plan. A voice inside me said, "You need to make another call." So I stopped under a streetlight and looked at my list of names. Once again that inner voice said, "Go see that one." It was not the name I would have picked out. The address on the card was in the opposite direction from our home and several miles away. But I went. About fifteen minutes later, I knocked on the door of an apartment and introduced myself. After I told the man I was calling on behalf of our church, he said to me, "You won't believe this, but about fifteen minutes ago (about the time I was sitting under the streetlight), my wife and I were sitting at the supper table, and I told her that I wished someone would come by and explain to us how you go about becoming a Christian. Can you help us?"

You may call it a coincidence. I know better. The Holy Spirit planned a meeting and saw to it that the people who were supposed to be there were there. If something like this had happened once, I might have a very slight doubt, but similar experiences have occurred through the years. God frequently uses His Spirit in leading people to salvation.

One of the main functions of the Spirit is to help you. At the Last Supper, the last meal Jesus and His disciples shared just before His arrest and crucifixion, Jesus was trying to explain what was going to happen. John 16 tells this story. Take time now to read it.

The seventh verse tells us that Jesus told them that when He went away He would send "the Comforter." He was speaking of the Holy Spirit. And in John 14:16, He tells them He will send "another comforter." The word "another" in Greek (*allos*) means "another but similar." The Spirit is much like Christ, but in a different spiritual form. Jesus promised His disciples that they would still have God with them in the Spirit.

The second chapter of the Book of Acts tells of the Spirit coming to the disciples and the dramatic changes He made in their lives. They immediately began sharing the story of salvation, and one of the things the Spirit did was to enable them to speak in different languages so even those who did not speak Aramaic or Hebrew, the common languages of that area, still could understand. This was a gift of the Spirit.

Even today, we have people who translate the Bible into languages that have never been reduced to writing. The Wycliffe translators go into the jungles of Central and South America, and with the help of the Holy Spirit, they reduce the spoken language of a native tribe to an alphabet and then translate the Bible for them.

Now look at Acts 2:38. Peter tells all of those listening that if they repent and are baptized for the forgiveness of their sins, they will receive the gift of the Holy Spirit. So how does this affect us?

Very simply. If we will turn our lives over to God and trust Him for everything, He will fill us with the Holy Spirit to guide and direct our lives and to comfort us when we are hurting. When people become a Christian, the Holy Spirit resides in them. That is a promise from God. What is even more important is that when we yield our lives to God, the Spirit is then free to control our lives, enabling us to do God's will. Unfortunately, many people don't reach that point. They make a profession of faith, get baptized, and then keep on living the same old way they've always lived. They sin as a matter of course and continue to worry and be unhappy about the same old things.

Look at Ephesians 1:13-14. Paul says the Holy Spirit is God's down payment or pledge, guaranteeing eternal life to believers. When we believe in Him, He makes that deposit of the Holy Spirit in us as a guarantee.

Most Christians never appropriate this tremendous gift in the way they should. God wants to bless our lives, but if we continue to go about business as usual, the Spirit will not control our lives, and we lose this great benefit. In chapters 5 & 6 we will discuss in more detail how God expects us to live our lives. But to receive the full blessing of the Holy Spirit, we must completely yield ourselves to God. That is not done without working at it.

I have heard Christians blame God for what goes wrong in their lives. But when you ask them if they are completely yielded to Him, if they are studying God's Word and praying daily, and if they are letting the Spirit control their lives, the answer is almost always no. God does not intervene in our lives unless He is invited to. Most of us have a tendency to try to run our own lives until something goes wrong, and then we start blaming God because we have problems.

Let's look at some other things the Holy Spirit does. John 16:12-15 tells us that the Spirit will teach us. Read those verses now. Jesus is talking to the disciples and telling them that the things they don't understand now will be made clear by the Spirit in the days ahead. And He does the same for us. You will find that no matter how young or old you might be, as you start your Christian life, there is always more to learn. I feel sorry for those who never open their Bible except maybe on Sunday. This is one way God speaks to us through the Spirit, and we miss those blessings if we don't study His Word daily. The Holy Spirit wants to be our teacher and help us understand God's will for our lives. He wants to lead us to other Scriptures, another person, a Christian book, a sermon, or a Sunday school lesson that makes clear something we did not understand fully. We mentioned earlier that the Spirit inspired the writing of the Bible. Therefore, who is better to depend on to guide us through our study of His Word than He who helped author it?

Now open your Bible to Romans, and let's take a quick look at some other activities of the Spirit. The eighth chapter, verse fourteen, says that the Spirit will lead us. We are God's children, and if we let the Spirit control our life, He can lead us to make right decisions. Who wouldn't want a guide like that?

Move two verses down to verse sixteen, and you will find that the Spirit assures us that we are indeed God's children. When you are feeling discouraged and you go to God's Word, you suddenly find a verse of encouragement, or a little voice inside of you that says, "God loves you. Cheer up!" Or you suddenly feel the urge to call someone and they answer by saying, "Oh, I'm so glad you called. I was really feeling down today, and your call has perked me up." That is the Spirit working.

Go down to verse 26 in the same chapter. Read the rest of the chapter. What an encouragement! The Spirit is going to help us in our prayers. I particularly like verse 31, don't you?

There is one last thing about the Spirit, which we have already alluded to. The Spirit gives us spiritual gifts. That doesn't mean positions, wealth, or title. What it does mean is that He gives us gifts to make us more effective Christians. There are several references to spiritual gifts in your Bible. 1 Corinthians, chapter 12, is a good place for us to look. What he is saying here is that there is much work to be done by Christians, and if you seek His will, He will help you get that work done. To do that, He gives gifts of administration, teaching, preaching, taking care of the children, praying, greeting and so on. If you will give him the opportunity, the Spirit will also reveal your spiritual gift to you.

Something we don't talk much about in Baptist circles is the gift of speaking in tongues. There are some denominations that base part of their worship on this gift. I am not referring to speaking in a foreign tongue. What I am talking about here is speaking strange utterances that most people don't understand. The only reason I mention this is that there are some who teach that if you don't speak in tongues, you have not had the blessing of the Holy Spirit. This is not true. One of the problems with this kind of thinking is that "speaking in tongues" can become a matter of pride—"I've got something you don't have." I had a man tell me one time that I had not been filled with the Spirit because I did not speak in tongues. It upset me for a few days until I studied spiritual gifts in the Bible for myself and found that what he said was not true. God's word says that when I became a Christian, I became filled with the Spirit. Let me call your attention to chapter 14 in 1 Corinthians. It makes it plain that when speaking in tongues becomes a matter of pride, it is sinful. The only time when speaking in tongues really matters is when it edifies or builds up the church.

Don't let anyone say you haven't been filled with the Spirit because you don't speak in tongues. There are other gifts that are much more important. If you will seek to discover the gift that God has granted you, and then use it to the best of your ability, you will always please God.

We have just looked at the tip of the iceberg in our discussion of the Holy Spirit. If you are ready to learn more, you can look in your concordance in the back of your Bible and read some of the other references about the Holy Spirit. The Spirit is a very important Person of the Trinity, and therefore should be a very important part of your life as a Christian.

You may want to come back and read this chapter again in a few weeks. It will help clarify your understanding of who the Holy Spirit is and what He does.

CHAPTER 3

The Holy Bible

I have no way of knowing how familiar you are with the Bible. Some who read this may have already experienced considerable study in the Bible. Others may know very little about the Bible. Some Christians can quickly find any reference in the Bible. If they have a problem or a discussion with someone and they want to find a particular verse, they have the ability to turn to it very readily.

Others fumble around while looking in the table of contents or thumbing through their Bible. A frustrated look comes on their faces when the pastor announces where to turn for that day's Scripture. If it is a book they are not familiar with, they will try unobtrusively to hide their Bible under a hymnbook or their coat. The goal of this chapter is to acquaint you with your Bible and how to know what is available in it. We will talk more about the use of your Bible later on. I believe that all Christians ought to have a working knowledge of God's Word. They should be able to find verses, know where the Bible came from, and be able to use it in sharing with others. I believe this is the minimum that God expects from us.

Do not stay ignorant about how to use God's Word. If you will study this chapter carefully and do the things suggested, it should be very helpful to you and make your Bible a very worthwhile tool for your use. If you were going to have to go into the courtroom, you would either want to know all the ramifications of the law or hire an attorney who knew these things. Our walk with God is much more important than that—all the more reason to know what God's Book of directions and rules has to say to us.

Let's start with your Bible. If you don't have one, you need to acquire one immediately. You cannot really get much out of this book, or your Christian experience, without a Bible. Most bookstores carry Bibles. I would recommend Christian bookstores. They will usually have a large selection. You need to get familiar with where to go to find all kinds of good Christian reading materials.

If you cannot afford to buy a Bible, don't be shy about asking your church to provide one for you. Almost any pastor can put his hands on a copy that he can at least loan you. It may not have all the helps in it, but it can get you started. Meanwhile, you can start saving to buy one or perhaps put it on your wish list for a birthday or Christmas.

You will find there are many different translations of God's Word. If you ask someone else's opinion, you'll notice that everyone has a favorite. Many believers are persuaded their translation is the only one for you. Here is some information to help you decide.

The original Bible was written by many people through the inspiration of the Holy Spirit. It was written in Hebrew and Greek and a small portion in Aramaic. You and I will never see the original manuscripts. Down through the years, scholarly men and women have translated the Bible into many of the languages of the world. In fact, that work is still going on in parts of the world where a small tribe has its own language. Even in more developed areas of the world, new translations of the Bible appear quite frequently. So when we go out to buy a Bible, we want to buy a good translation that is dependable, readable, and understandable. To know which translation you are looking at, look at the spine of the cover or on the first pages. In today's world the New King James Version and the New International Version are the most popular for people who read English.

The original King James Version was translated in the 1600s, and many of the words and phrases reflect the spoken word of those days. The New King James Version is more readable. The New International Version is also very readable. Some people prefer the New Revised Standard Version. Pick up a copy of each. Read a few verses in two or three different places and then choose the one you prefer. You will also see some people who carry a Living Bible. This is a paraphrase, not a translation. It was put into modern English by a father who wanted a more understandable Bible for his children. It is very readable, but I would encourage you to start with the New International or New King James Version. You may want to purchase a Living Bible later to use in devotional times, or to check on some verses that may not be clear to you.

In a good Christian bookstore you will find several other translations. Some are just the New Testament. You will want to have both the Old and New Testaments in your first Bible. It would be helpful if you have a version that many other people in your church and Bible study classes are using. As you mature in your Christian growth, you can add other translations to your study table.

There are some other decisions to make before you buy a Bible. Some of the Bibles you look at will say "Red Letter," or you may notice in leafing through that there are some words in red print. These are the words of Jesus. This is nice to have, but there are other helps I feel will be of more benefit to you.

You will find some Bibles are designated on the box or the cover as a "Study Bible." The box or the Bible itself may have the name of the person who has added some comments to God's Word. This means that a person schooled in the Scriptures has written some study helps so that you might better understand what you read. These helps are not a part of God's inspired or Holy Word. These comments will usually be at the bottom of each page. This can be very helpful, but I would recommend that if you go this route, that you talk with your pastor about which study Bible to purchase. Many of these will be in more than one translation.

Another item that is a tremendous help is a concordance. In the back of the Bible will be a listing of words similar to that in a dictionary. By each word will be part of a sentence with the Scripture reference where it is found. This enables you to look up a topic or a word and find the particular verses that relate to that topic or word. A concordance is particularly helpful when you study, and ought to be in your new Bible.

Good maps are also helpful. Your Bible mentions various countries and cities. Geography sometimes plays an important part in understanding the story. It is nice to be able to look at the maps in your Bible and see exactly where those places are located. Look at Paul's Missionary Journeys, a map that is common in many Bibles. Then remember that all of his travel was done on foot or by small sailing ships. A map can help you to begin to appreciate how much this man was willing to undertake, and the physical stamina required, in his efforts to spread God's Word.

Before we move on, let me mention just a couple more items. In a good Bible you will find a column of small print down the outside margins or down the center column of each page. You will notice that there are small numbers or letters that refer to the Scripture on that page. Then it provides references to related Scriptures on the same topic found in other parts of the Bible. This is a great help in studying.

In the front of the Bible there should be a Table of Contents. This will tell you many of the things that are in your Bible. The Bible I use even has a "Synopsis of Bible Doctrine"; "The Inspiration of the Bible"; "Understanding The Bible"; and "How We Got Our Bible" as added features to those I have mentioned. Compare the Table of Contents in two or three Bibles by different publishers to get the most for your money. Then you are ready to make a decision on which Bible best fits your needs. Later on, you may want to put on your wish list some other translations, a Bible Dictionary, or other study materials.

Now that you have your Bible, let's look at what's there. We have already talked about concordances, maps, and other helps and aids. What I want to explain to you next are the basics.

Your Bible is composed of an Old Testament and a New Testament. The Old Testament was written before Christ was born and tells the story of the Jewish people. It begins with the story of the creation of the world and contains some tremendous stories about people who trusted in God long before the coming of Jesus and His sacrifice on the cross for us.

OLD TESTAMENT

The Old Testament is made up of thirty-nine different books written by many authors. Each one of these authors was divinely inspired by God through the Holy Spirit to write God's message for His people. Then, over a period of many years, God led various men to bring these books together until the Bible in its entirety was compiled.

In 1947, a shepherd boy in an area just above the Dead Sea threw a rock into a cave and was surprised to hear pottery breaking. He went into the cave and found ancient scrolls on parchment, rolled and placed in clay jars. Further exploration uncovered more of these scrolls in nearby caves. These are now referred to as the Dead Sea Scrolls, and they authenticate much of the Old Testament.

The thirty-nine books of the Old Testament are divided into five sections. The first section is history books, spelling out the history of the Jewish people. This section is sometimes called the Pentateuch, or the books of The Law. These books were written by Moses and include a total of five books: Genesis, the story of creation; Exodus, the story of the Jewish people in captivity in Egypt; Leviticus, which is a thorough coverage of the Jewish law; and then Numbers and Deuteronomy, which detail the wandering of the Jewish people after their exodus from Egypt.

The next section contains twelve more books of history that cover the kingdom of Israel being established and the Hebrew people's later captivity by the Babylonians.

These are followed by five books of poetry. The most popular of these is the book of Psalms. Also included is the book of Proverbs. It is a book of wisdom that is well worth reading.

The next five books are called the Major Prophets, and directly after are the twelve books called the Minor Prophets. They prophesy, among other things, the coming of the Messiah. As well, there are prophecies of things yet to come. So don't ever let anyone tell you that the Old Testament is not important or worth studying. It deserves your attention.

NEW TESTAMENT

The New Testament contains twenty-seven books and tells of Christ's birth and life and the lives of the early Christians who lived during the first century after Christ. The New Testament is also divided into sections. The first four books are called the Gospels, and they tell of Christ's life and ministry. These are followed by Acts, a history of the early church. Then there are two sets of Epistles (letters). The first group are the Pauline Epistles, which are letters written by Paul to various early Christian churches and individuals. There are thirteen of these. These are followed by the book of Hebrews. We are not certain who is the author of this book, but we know it was written to the Hebrew people. There are seven General Epistles that follow. These are named for the authors instead of being named for the recipients like the Pauline Epistles.

J. Sidlow Baxter, a noted Bible scholar, divides them differently. He says there are nine Christian Church Epistles (Romans to 2 Thessalonians) and four Pastoral and Personal Epistles (1 Timothy to Philemon). Finally, there are nine Hebrew Christian Epistles (Hebrews to Revelation). He believes more emphasis should be made on studying the Christian Church and Pastoral and Personal Epistles. He says that these books are "written to us and profitable for us."[1] The last book in the Bible is the book of Revelation (don't put an s on Revelation), which describes the triumph of Christ when He comes again.

There is a lot more that could be said about the Bible, but this is enough to get us started on a journey of study that will, we hope, continue until the time comes to be in His presence.

Now let's try out that new Bible. Turn to 2 Timothy 3:16-17. Read those verses while I wait for you. Then turn back a couple of pages to 2 Timothy 2:15. Do you see your responsibility to study, to learn, and to understand God's Word so that you can do His will? It will take a strong commitment to study the Bible diligently.

There are lots of different opinions on how to go about studying this tremendous book. The most important thing to remember is to study every day. Set aside a definite time, a half hour or so, and faithfully study. Start today! Then, as you work though this book of New Beginnings, you will be given various Bible passages to study that will be helpful to you in getting some basics.

As soon as you have finished this textbook, I encourage you to start reading the Bible through from the first page to the last and to set a goal to read it all within one year. Set a pace that you can follow. Your church or a Christian bookstore can provide you with a plan to do this. It may be as simple as reading four or five pages each morning, or it may involve reading some from the New Testament and the Old Testament each day. Whatever the plan, stick to it, and you will be amazed at what you will learn. We will discuss how to go about this in more detail in chapters 6 & 7.

Endnotes

1   J. Sidlow Baxter, *Explore the Book:* (Zondervan Publishing, 1964), pp. 53-59.

CHAPTER 4

Why Do I Need to Go to Church?

Before we talk about going to church, we need to define what the church is. There is a lot of misunderstanding regarding that. Most of us have a habit of referring to the church as that big red-brick building close to downtown, or the white-frame building with the cross on top of the steeple out in the country, or the modern stone and brick complex of buildings that we attend each Sunday.

When Christ lived, His Jewish countrymen attended the synagogue, and they still do today. As people started to follow Jesus and found there was more to following God than what was offered at the synagogue, there was a natural inclination to want to meet together with fellow Christians. The same thing happens today. A group of Christians get to know one another in a neighborhood or community. There isn't a building readily available to meet in, so they meet in someone's home. The next step might be to rent a school building to meet in on Sunday morning or a warehouse or empty storefront or perhaps even an occupied store. I know of a large church in Dallas that started meeting in a carpet store that belonged to one of the members. The school or store where people meet is not the church. And neither is that big red-brick building with the pews, a pipe organ, and a steeple with a cross on the top.

The church is a group of Christian believers who meet together to worship and praise God. It doesn't matter what kind of a building they meet in, or if they meet in the park. The people are the church: the buildings are only places to meet in. I wrote the history of the First Baptist Church in Marble Falls, Texas, for its one-hundredth anniversary. That church had its first meeting in the city park, where the people sat on a pile of railroad ties. In Tanzania, I met with several groups of Christians back in the bush. As we worshiped we met out of doors, and most of the people sat on the ground.

We have a tendency to place too much emphasis on buildings. The important thing is the people. They are the church. They are what God is interested in. When you meet to worship God with a group of fellow Christians on a regular basis, then you are the church. In chapter 11, we will talk about how churches are organized and constituted. But don't confuse the buildings where you meet with what the church really is.

The disciples in Jesus' time met in homes. In Romans 16:5, Paul mentions the church that met at the house of Priscilla and Aquila. Acts 20 tells of the Christian people meeting at Troas. It doesn't tell us what kind of a building they used, but we do know that it had three floors. We know this because Eutychus fell asleep during the sermon and fell out of the third-story window. He survived to tell about it. It is plain to see that churches did not always meet in what we today would call a conventional church building.

My wife and I volunteered to spend two years working for the Canadian Southern Baptist Seminary. When we got to Canada, I was asked to pastor a small church in Calgary. It met in a school library. Every Sunday we had to move out all of the library tables, set up the chairs, roll in the piano and a lectern, put out hymnbooks, and then take it all back down when we were finished. We used a couple of classrooms and the teacher's lounge for our Bible studies.

Another church in Calgary met in the top of the Olympic ski jump tower. Its members had a long elevator ride but were rewarded with a beautiful view.

As you can see, where we meet is not important. What is important is that Christian people meet together on a regular basis to worship and praise God.

Now let's look at some reasons we need to go to church. The most important reason to attend is that God instructed us to. Open your Bible to Hebrews 10:21-25. Read those five verses while I wait for you.

Do you grasp what God is saying? There's a lot there! Christ is our Great (or High) Priest. He is our door key to the House of God. How foolish it would be for us to ignore this opportunity to commune with God through Jesus. God gave His Son for us to be able to enter the Holy place, and yet some never come near to pray or to give thanks. These verses say we ought to be unswerving in our faith because He was faithful to us. How do we do this? Verse 25 says don't neglect (don't give up, forsake not) meeting or assembling together. Some people may be neglecting worshiping together, but if they had a glimmer of what God has done for them and what He expects from them, they would meet together and encourage one another toward love and good deeds.

Christians also meet together to worship God because He is worthy of our worship. He created us. He gave us everything we have. He saved us through the sacrifice of His Son. Why would we not want to worship Him? Do we not all spend time in a lot of other activities that are not nearly as worthy? God certainly deserves more than the few hours or minutes a week that we give to Him.

I won't make you look up these Scriptures, but I'll give you their main theme. However, I recommend that you get in a little practice by finding them in your Bible and reading these entire verses. If you choose to do so, I'll wait for you.

Joshua 22:27 says in part, "We will worship the Lord at His sanctuary….Then in the future your descendants will not be able to say to ours, 'You have no share in the Lord.'"

Psalm 95:6— "Come, let us bow down in worship."

Psalm 100:2— "Worship the Lord with gladness."

Matthew 4:10— "Worship the Lord, your God, and serve Him only."

John 4:24— "God is spirit and His worshipers must worship Him in spirit and in truth." A study Bible says the English word "worship" was originally spelled "worthship" and means to acknowledge the worth of the object worshiped. We acknowledge God's worth in spirit (in contrast to material ways) and in truth (in contrast to falsehood).

God's Word is quite plain in saying that we are to worship Him. I have had people say to me, "Well, I can worship God out in a field hunting or on the lake fishing just as well as you can in church." And that is partially true. When you are in a spot of beauty—a lake, a woods, or a mountaintop—it is a great place to worship God. But first of all, there has to be more than the thought that "I can." The act of worship must take place. Secondly, this does not meet the requirement of "assembling yourselves together to encourage…." Every Sunday morning on our way to church, we drive across a two-mile-long bridge that crosses a lake. I have yet to see any of the many fishermen in their boats where it appeared that they were taking time to worship God.

If we look once again at the first-generation Christians, we read in Acts 2:41-44 that they met together to worship God, to be baptized, to pray, to study His Word together, and to celebrate the Lord's Supper together. It concludes by saying, "All believers were seen together." Being together is hard to do by yourself.

Therefore, we must realize up front that one of our primary reasons for worshiping together is that God instructs us to do so. We have made a commitment that says we want to please Him as well. Let's look at some other good reasons for us to worship together.

Several years ago I met a man in church one Sunday morning. He had recently moved to the town where we lived. I found out his wife had passed away a few years before, and he had decided to retire in our community. We became friends and rejoiced with him when he re-married a few months later to a Christian lady from West Texas. We had good times going to dinner after church, playing golf, and visiting in each other's homes. Although we now live 150 miles apart, we still visit each other and talk on the phone. We have been friends for many years.

As we got to know them, Alton and I learned we could confide in each other and depend on each other when we needed assistance or prayers. I looked forward to seeing Alton and Marie on each visit. He had a heart problem one evening while visiting us, and we sat with his wife through long hours at the hospital until he recovered.

Friendships, like my friendship with Alton, mean a lot to most of us. One of the great places for making those kinds of friends is in church. We enjoy Alton and Marie's company because, when the four of us go out to dinner or to each other's home, we never have to be concerned about getting into an uncomfortable situation. Because they feel the same way about Christ as we do, we don't have to be concerned with problems like alcoholic drinks, dirty stories, foul language, or flirting with someone else's spouse.

I spent many years in the life insurance and real estate businesses and had to go to many conventions and business meetings where some or all of these problems were always present. I'm not a prude. I enjoy a good time as much as anyone, but God expects Christians to have certain moral standards. The reason He expects us to live according to His standards is that one can't really be a witness to someone else about his Christian life if that life does not reflect the influence of Christ in the way that he lives.

Where do I learn how to live according to His will? In the worship and Bible study services at church. It is very important that we go to worship and that we cultivate some Christian friends to encourage us and pray with us and for us. Church is not just a place to meet other people with similar moral values. It does offer us an opportunity to develop some Christian friends. It also is a teaching ground for us to learn how to live our lives so that we will please God.

You are going to face problems at various points in your life. For many, this will happen more than once. Your parents get old and frail. You may have business or health problems, or your children have difficulties. These are times when it really helps to have friends to stand by you or just pray for your situation. If God's people know about these situations, you can always count on them for help. If you never go near the church or only attend on Christmas and Easter, they never get to know you, and you never get to know them. And there are times when you will need a close friend.

Earlier I mentioned our daughter's bout with cancer. During her long illness, friends from church stood by us, visited the hospital, came to our home, and prayed for Helen's healing. Outside of those church people, I could count on the fingers of one hand the people who showed any concern. I was glad we had made good friends in our church.

Another less obvious reason for going to church relates to our discussion in the second chapter concerning spiritual gifts. In 1 Corinthians 12, there is a long discourse on spiritual gifts. Look at verse twelve. "The body (you will find the church referred to as 'the body of Christ') is a unit, though it is made up of many parts; and though all its parts are many, they form one body."

Then read verses 14-31. Let me call your attention particularly to verses 27-28. "Now you are the body of Christ, and each one of you is a part of it. And in the church God has appointed first of all apostles, second prophets, third teachers, then workers of miracles, also those having gifts of healing, those able to help others, those with gifts of administration, and those speaking in different kinds of tongues."

Let me ask you: if this is true, then how can the body of Christ operate efficiently when some of its members only show up at Christmas, others once every five or six weeks, and some not at all? If God has given us gifts to help build the church, don't we have a responsibility to participate in that work?

If you want to know (and I hope you do) what God really wants His church to be like, look at 1 Thessalonians 1:1-10. Read it now. Why does Paul say he thanks God for the members of the Thessalonica church? Look at verse three again. "Your work produced by faith, your labor prompted by love, and your endurance inspired by hope in our Lord Jesus Christ" And in verse four, "The gospel came to you not simply by words, but also with power, with the Holy Spirit and with deep conviction." Then in verse six, "You became imitators of us and of the Lord, in spite of severe suffering. You welcomed the message with joy. And so you became a model to all the believers in Macedonia and Achaia. The Lord's message rang out from you...your faith in God has become known everywhere. They tell how you turned to God from idols to serve the living and true God, and to wait for His Son from heaven."

What a testimony to this little struggling church! Could Paul say that about the church you attend, or the one I attend? If that is to be said of any of today's churches, we have a lot to live up to, and it will only happen if we do our share to make it happen.

One thing I have always liked about Baptists is our Bible

study time. Almost every Christian group has Bible study for youngsters, while some denominations have Bible study for adults. In some churches the kids go to Sunday school while the parents go to worship. The parents lose out on the time to get in a small group with people their own age to study God's Word. They don't have the opportunity to relate God's Word to their lives. This is not a part of the worship hour, but usually takes place either just before or afterward. In some churches it may be on a weekday evening or a Saturday.

Don't let the name Sunday school be a turnoff. Some relate the name to a children's activity. But Sunday school or Bible study is for everyone. You need to be in Bible study each week. I have been going to Bible study or Sunday school for more years than most of you have been alive. I have taught Sunday school for over forty years, but there has never been a Sunday, that in studying to teach I haven't learned something new. The same thing will be true for you. If you attend Sunday school faithfully, study the lesson, and pay attention to the teacher, I guarantee you that you will learn things from the Bible that will help you for the rest of your life.

Let me add one note here about Sunday school and church. I have had people say to me, "I won't ever take my kids to church or Sunday school. My parents took me when I was growing up, and I want my kids to make their own decisions."

Then I ask them, "Didn't your folks ever take you to a ball game, or the movies, or out for ice cream? Do you also deny those pleasures to your kids?"

One more thing we need to mention. I assume most of you have already joined a church, but there may be some who need to join and don't know how. It would be great if each of you had a Christian friend to be your mentor. It would be good if someone is encouraging you to attend church each Sunday.

There are probably some of you who had this book given to you by a church member that cares about you and wants to see you become a disciple of Jesus Christ. If that is the case, then the church where that person belongs is where you ought to belong. Having a Christian friend to guide you is very important for growing in spiritual maturity.

If you picked this book up at a bookstore or it was given to you by a friend in another city, and you haven't had contact with a local church, then you need to look for a nearby church where God's Word is preached and obeyed. That is difficult for a new Christian to ascertain. Yet, if you attend a couple of Sundays and you notice in the worship service or Bible study that most people are using their Bible, you can feel fairly certain that it is a place where you can learn God's Word and worship Him. Being close to where you live is not the most important thing, but it does help you to be able to attend more services and make more friends. Listen carefully to what is taught and preached. Any church that uses a book or training materials that are not directly related to the Bible or that do not use Scripture references as its main item of study is probably not the best place for you to belong. I would urge you to try to find a Southern Baptist church if there is one in your community.

Now, how do you join? In most Southern Baptist churches, the pastor will give you the opportunity to join at the conclusion of each worship service. He will give what is called an "invitation" after his message. He will specify that this is the time to come forward. Then the congregation will usually sing a hymn. When this occurs, you simply walk down the aisle and tell the pastor that you are a new Christian and that you want to join that church. He will pray with you, introduce you to the congregation, and the church will accept you as a new member. Afterward, someone will contact you about being baptized. This means you will be immersed in the baptistery at the church, or in some cases at another location. We will talk about baptism in detail in chapter 9. Be sure you read that chapter so that you completely understand the significance of the ordinance of baptism of the church.

Once you have been baptized, and happen to move or are transferred to another city, or even across a large city, you can join the local church by transferring your membership. You don't need to worry too much about the details. You may hear someone refer to it as transferring your letter. When you get ready to transfer, you simply go to the front at the invitation time in the new church and tell the pastor or staff member that you want to transfer your membership. He will take care of all the details. Pastors and staff members in almost every church are very willing to talk to you about joining their church. You can simply call the church office on a weekday and ask to make an appointment to speak with one of them.

Don't neglect regular worship and Bible study. If you move, transfer your letter as soon as possible. Whether you stay in one city all of your life or move ten times, be active in your church. Analyze your strong points to see what gifts God has given to you, and then put those gifts to work in your local church. That is how you will find happiness in serving Him.

CHAPTER 5

Repentance

At the time of writing this book, sin is making the headlines in a big way. And there is some debate as to what the definition of sin is. The dictionary says sin is to "err, or go astray." To a Christian, to sin is to go against God's will, to go astray in serving Him.

We may have a tendency to try and grade sin. We think of someone being more sinful because they kill someone or commit adultery, or we may tend to condemn them because of the number of times they sin.

We must remember that we are not the judge. God is the judge. Matthew 7:1 warns us, "Do not judge or you too will be judged." It is easier to judge someone else than to look at our own sins. But we do sin, and there is a need for repentance in our lives.

Romans 3:23 says, "For all have sinned and fall short of the glory of God." When it says "all," that includes me, it includes you, it includes every one of us. We have a tendency to get so wrapped up in reading about and discussing the sins of others that we tend to get complacent about our own lives.

Sin has been making the headlines, and the newspapers, television commentators, politicians, and we the people are all absorbed with it, because it is not our sin. It has always been more exciting to talk about other people and their sin, to criticize others for their misgivings, than it is to look at our own sins and shortcomings.

But Confucius or someone (I have a friend who credits Pete Boudreau, his Cajun classmate with all such sayings) says, "People who live in glass houses shouldn't throw rocks." Jesus also used "rocks" in His comments about looking to ourselves first in His defense of the prostitute. He said, "If anyone of you is without sin let him be the first to throw at stone at her" (John 8:7).

Proverbs 30:12 says, "There are those who are pure in their own eyes and yet are not cleansed of their filth." Most of us, if we are honest, find ourselves in that description at times. So for the next few minutes, as you read this chapter, forget the sins of anyone else. Think about the fact that all of us do some things that displease God. Then let's look at what we can do to make it right with God. That's what repentance is all about.

When we became a Christian we acknowledged that we were sinners. Read Romans 6:1-14. The death it talks about is the death of our old life when we became a Christian. It says we should not take advantage of God's grace by continuing to sin.

God will help us to turn from sin as explained in Acts 20:21, where it says, "I have declared to both Jews and Greeks that they must turn to God in repentance and have faith in our Lord Jesus." When we prayed to receive Jesus, we told Him that we were a sinner and asked for Him to come into our life and to forgive us.

But we continue to sin. That is why, when Jesus gave us the Lord's Prayer, He outlined in that pattern a continuing request for forgiveness of our sins. "Forgive us our debts, as we also have forgiven our debtors. And lead us not into temptation, but deliver us from the evil one" (Matthew 6: 12-13). Our "debts" are obligations incurred, that is, sins of omission and commission. Jesus says we need to pray to ask forgiveness for those obligations. And this brings us to repentance.

In Acts 2:38, Peter tells the crowd to whom he is preaching, "Repent and be baptized, every one of you, in the name of Jesus Christ for the forgiveness of your sins."

John the Baptist also talked about repentance in Matthew 3:2. "Repent, for the kingdom of heaven is at hand." And just a few verses later, in Matthew 4:17, Matthew says, "From that time on Jesus began to preach, 'Repent, for the kingdom of heaven is near.'" In Luke 13:3 and again in verse five, Jesus says, "Unless you repent, you too will perish."

Move over to the book of Mark, and you find the disciples preaching the same thing. "They went out and preached that people should repent" (Mark 6:12).

Doesn't it make you begin to think that God was serious about repentance? It was important in the Old Testament, which we will look at in a moment, and it was important in the New Testament, which we have just seen. There is no reason to assume it is any less important today. When we sin, God expects us to repent. He doesn't leave us an option. He doesn't say, "If it bothers you a lot, maybe you ought to repent." Or, "If you stack up a whole bunch of sins, you might want to think of repentance." When we become aware that we are doing something wrong, we need to ask for forgiveness and repent, starting right then.

Now, let's look at repentance and get a good understanding of what we mean by the word. The dictionary says that to repent is to turn around and go in the opposite direction. Remember, we said that sin was to go astray. So if we are going to repent, we need to get back on the right track. This is very important. It is not to just say we're sorry. It is to change direction. Why is that so important?

Read Romans 2:1-13. I'll wait for you. Read it through a couple of times. Repentance starts when we become a Christian. If we have bad habits, if we are doing immoral things, we need to stop doing them, turn around, and go the other way. After we become a Christian, if we slip into a bad habit, whether it is gossiping, lying, stealing, using drugs, illicit sex, whatever it is, we must repent. We have to turn in another direction, if we want to please God, and that should be our goal.

Chuck Swindoll, president of Dallas Theological Seminary, in his book about David, talks of our awareness of sin being like the warning light on the dashboard of our car. If I'm driving down the highway and suddenly a red light shines out at me from the dash, I am aware that there is some kind of problem with my car. One thing I can do is just ignore it. Maybe I can shift around a little and get the steering wheel between me and the light so I don't see it. Sometimes that's hard to do. It is shining right in my face. So I reach in the glove box, pull out a small hammer, and bash the light out and keep on driving. It no longer shines in my face, so everything is now all right. WRONG!

Nothing may happen for a while. Whether I have blocked it out of my mind, or smashed the warning signal, I can probably go on for a few miles. Then the engine burns up, and suddenly I look back and realize what a foolish decision I made to ignore the warning light.

It's like life. I start out to do something that I think may bring me enjoyment. It may bring me a lot of pleasure, but the warning sign goes off inside me. I wake up some night with the thought, "What if I get caught? What if someone says something? What if___?" That's God, turning on the warning signal.

I can probably take out my little hammer, smash out the warning signal, or change my view by saying, "Well, everyone else is doing it," or "What I am doing is not so bad, at least not as bad as ____." There are always lots of good excuses for doing wrong. We are just red-blooded Americans, right?

The warning sign says, "THIN ICE," but I'll stay close to the edge. The ice is probably thicker than it appears. I'll be okay."

Maybe no one ever will see me or catch me. Maybe I can get away with it. But the worry is still there. And if I do get caught, consider the consequences. Also remember, God knows, even if no one else does. Stop and read Hebrews 4:13.

Speaking of consequences, my heart aches for the millions of kids caught up in the tragedy of broken homes, which is one of the consequences of sin. Divorce, prison, loss of employment, loss of friends, embarrassment, all cause lots of grief for other family members. If you don't believe me, just go to the airport near you on a Sunday evening and watch the migration. Kids, eight, ten, or twelve years old are saying tearful good-byes to a mom or a dad before boarding a plane to go home. On the other end, a mom, dad, or stepdad is waiting to pick up kids who have been with the other parent over the weekend. Talk to them. They are hurting inside. They feel an allegiance to their parents, yet they don't want to miss out on the things happening at school or with their friends. What a tragedy, and quite often it is caused by a parent who has sinned and refuses to repent.

It isn't always a sexual sin. It can be a dishonest business dealing, habitual lying, or one of the biggest causes, mismanagement of money. It is still a sin.

I'm not saying that every sin ends up with a broken family. That is just one of the tragedies of sin. We can ruin our health with sin. We can destroy our reputation with sin. We can hurt many besides ourselves when we sin.

So when God turns on that little warning sign on the dashboard of life, don't smash it out with a hammer. Stop sinning, and turn in another direction. REPENT!

The Bible is full of stories of repentance. Solomon, in 1 Kings 8:46-51, prays to God, "If they have a change of heart....and repent.....and if they turn back to you...hear their prayer...and uphold their cause." Turn to it and read the whole thing. Solomon realized the importance of the people turning back to God, if they expected God to forgive them.

Second Chronicles 19:4 tells us that King Jehosophat "went out again among the people... and turned them back to the Lord." Move over to 2 Chronicles 28:9-15 and read how repentance works. The soldiers aren't told to "just say you're sorry." They were given instructions, and they "provided them with clothes and sandals, food and drink, and healing balm. All those who were weak they put on donkeys." Do you see the difference? Repentance is not just being sorry. It is making amends. It is breaking bad habits. It is making a change in the direction of our lives.

I have been in revival meetings or preaching services where real repentance was experienced. True repentance will oftentimes result in brokeness, tears, expressions of forgiveness, or sorrow.

Repentance does not occur when a person says they are sorry and goes right on doing what they were doing; or blames their situation on someone else. We also need to remember that no one else can repent for us. My wife cannot repent for me. She knows most, if not all, of my sins. She can be God's tool in reminding me of my sins, as God used Nathan to remind David of his sin; but she can't repent for me. (See 2 Samuel 12.)

In 1 Corinthians 6:19, we are reminded, "Do you not know that your body is a temple of the Holy Spirit, who is in you?" Remember in chapter 2 we talked about the Holy Spirit, and how we are filled with Him when we become a Christian. This verse reminds us that because of that filling, we are the temple where the Holy Spirit resides. That brings us to the point that we need to be well aware of. We need to make every effort to keep that temple pure. We do not want the Holy Spirit of God residing in a dirty temple. So repentance has to include a thorough cleansing of the temple where the Spirit resides. 2 Chronicles 29 gives us a description of the cleansing of the temple, which should give you a pretty good idea of what we need to do to clean our temple. Consecration, purification, taking out everything unclean, and making up for unfaithfulness are all a part of cleansing and repentance.

Let me return to Chuck Swindoll's book on David and his failure with Bathsheba. I don't want to dwell on it because sexual sins are not the only ones that call for repentance. But the application applies to all the sins in our life.

David's failure to do his job started his problem. As king, he was supposed to be out with his army, but the Scriptures say he stayed at home. That was when his temptation came. And it can happen to us when we are not paying attention to our responsibilities at home or work.

While I was working at the Canadian Southern Baptist Seminary, we had a preacher at chapel service who advised the seminary students to wear blinders. Race horses and even work horses sometimes wear blinders so they won't be distracted. What was he saying? Don't put yourself in compromising situations. When you see temptation looming, or should I say luring on the horizon, turn the other way. If we continually look for temptation, we are bound to find it. If we wear revealing clothes (men or women), give "come hither looks," make suggestive remarks, tell off-color stories, tell "little" lies, steal little things, become envious of other people's possessions, feel we are just a little above the law, we are headed for trouble. It brought David trouble. It brought Bathsheba trouble. It will bring us trouble.

If David had been doing his job, out where he was supposed to be, he would never have seen Bathsheba. And if Bathsheba hadn't been bathing where the king could see her, the incident wouldn't have happened. The law in

Deuteronomy 17:17 told David that kings were not to "multiply wives, for himself lest his heart turn away." David didn't follow this edict. He had more than one wife and several concubines and wanted more. He disobeyed God's Word, his next step into trouble.

Successful and comfortable he neglects his duties, ignores God's Word, and trouble arrives. It is not unlike today. A man or woman does well and is proud of it. Soon they pay less and less attention to God's Word. They start neglecting their families in pursuit of pleasure, and temptation looms. "I'm doing good, nothing can hurt me!" And then the warning light goes on.

So one night of illicit love led to the siring of a child, which led to the child's death. One night of romance led to the murder of Bathsheba's husband. When it all sank in, it brought anguish to David, who carried guilt with him for the rest of his life. Yes, God forgave, but that didn't bring Uriah or the baby back. And for the rest of David's life, he and his family paid the consequences. "Why have you despised the word of the Lord by doing evil in His sight? You have struck down Uriah the Hittite with the sword; have taken his wife to be your wife, and have killed him with the sword of the sons of Ammon. 'Now, therefore, the sword will never depart from your house—Behold, I will raise up evil against you from your own household'" (2 Samuel 12).

Psalm 32:3-4 gives us some insight into David's guilt feelings. "When I kept silent about my sin, my body wasted away through my groaning all day long. For day and night thy hand was heavy upon me, my vitality was drained away as with the fever-heat of summer."

David repented. He did not escape the punishment. We never do. Repentance can't restore damage done, but true repentance starts the healing process.

Let's look at what Chuck Swindoll identifies as true repentance.

1. "There was open, unguarded admission. David said, 'I have sinned—-I have not hidden my sin.' No excuses— no hedging—no blaming anyone else. 'I HAVE SINNED AGAINST GOD!' When a person holds back the truth or tells you only part of it, he or she is not repentant."
2. "When there is true repentance there is a desire to make a complete break from sin. Repentance is turning around, on the basis of truth, and going in the opposite direction, making a complete break with what has been."

   Proverbs 28:13—He who conceals his transgressions will not prosper, but he who confesses and forsakes them will find compassion.
3. "When there is true repentance, the spirit is broken and humble. Psalm 51:17—'The sacrifices of God are a broken spirit; a broken and contrite heart, O God, thou wilt not despise.' It isn't a time to be defensive or angry, or proud, or bitter. A contrite heart makes no demand and has no expectations."
4. "True repentance is a claiming of God's forgiveness and reinstatement."[1]

One more thing and we'll move on. If we have truly repented, others will know it. Acts 26:20 spells it out. "First to those in Jerusalem and in all Judea, and to the Gentiles also, I preached that they should repent and turn to God and prove their repentance by their deeds."

Matthew 3:8 sums it up. "Produce fruit in keeping with repentance." In other words, do good with your life. Let others see Jesus in you.

You and I cannot afford to have unforgiven sin in our lives. The Holy Spirit can't work in a dirty temple, and we can't serve God with our best.

Check your life. Be honest with yourself. Ask God to forgive you for any sins you haven't confessed before. Then repent. Change direction. Get right with God and any injured parties, and then do your best to live your life in a way that is pleasing to God. The next chapter will help you to know what God expects.

Endnotes

1 Swindoll, Charles. David (Word, 1997), pp. 206-207.

CHAPTER 6

What Is Expected of Me As a Christian?

*T*his is a chapter you will probably want to refer to many times. You are now to the point that what you do next is very important. It is a lot like starting a new job. The first couple of weeks, you have people standing by to tell you almost every move to make. Then you come in one day and you are left pretty much on your own, and yet you still don't feel comfortable about what you are supposed to do. The same thing is true when we become Christians. We get some guidance for the first couple of steps, and then they put this book in your hands, or you buy it at the bookstore—and suddenly you are on your own without knowing quite what is expected of you.

I hope your church has assigned a mentor to work with you as you study this text and then to see that you are situated in a good Sunday school class—with someone who can answer your questions and help you grow spiritually. If you have not had someone assigned to you, ask your pastor if he would introduce you to someone who might be your mentor for a few weeks.

Some new Christians make a profession of faith and get baptized, and then for one reason or another they don't grow spiritually the way they should. Some even fail to attend church on a regular basis, and then their Christian life goes dormant.

They never mature as a Christian. They say they are Christian, but the moment anything gets the least bit off center in their lives, they blame all of the bad things on God. Or they turn back to some old habits that weren't good for them in the first place, or they just drop out. They may feel hopelessly confused or neglected, or both, or they may find it easier to drop back into their old lifestyle. DON'T DO IT! God expects more from us. And we should expect more from being a Christian.

God has a definite plan for our lives. He has made some great promises to us. We shouldn't short change ourselves. We will never be sorry if we do what God wants us to do, and if we understand how it will benefit us. This chapter is not just about what is expected of us, but also what we can expect from God.

There is one word that describes the relationship between ourselves and God and is an absolutely essential element in our relationship with God. I believe it shows where the vast majority of Christian people fall way short. It is the reason they don't experience all that God has for them. That word is **FAITH**. I mentioned this in the first chapter. We have to trust God "in faith" to start our Christian walk. We make a "profession of faith" to declare that we are a Christian. That is a very important start for us, but we must also go a lot deeper.

We do things by faith every day. We have faith that when we press the switch, the light will go on. We have faith that when we drive to the grocery store, it will be open, and that there will be bread and milk and fresh vegetables on the counters and shelves. We don't seem to have any problem in having faith that multitudes of people and dozens of pieces of machinery will operate efficiently day after day to provide elevator service, hot and cold water, traffic lights, and a myriad of other services we assume will be there. We never even give it a second thought. We take it by faith.

But when it comes to having faith in God to provide for us, we get skittish. I hope that if you get nothing else from this book, you will understand this one statement. *The biggest error most Christian people make is that they don't put their entire faith in God from day one.*

I speak from experience. I started going to church when I was two weeks old. My mother was responsible for what they called the Cradle Roll Department at our church. She took care of everyone's babies while they went to Sunday school and church. So it was easy for her to take me. I was just one more baby to take care of. When I was eight years old, I made a profession of faith and was baptized. As a child and as an adult, I have been in church almost every Sunday. I have taught Sunday school classes for over forty years. I have been a deacon (more about deacons in chapter 11) since I was twenty-four years old. I was ordained as a pastor a few years ago at the age of sixty-five. I have served on just about every committee at church.

The biggest mistake I ever made in my life was my failure to put my complete faith and trust in God for many of those years. I always felt confident that I could take care of myself. I was strong, healthy, received a good education, made a good living, and lived in a nice home. While our daughter Helen was ill, I drew closer to God, and then as she recovered, I gradually slid back into my self-reliance. It was only as I grew older that I realized what a big mistake I had made in not putting all of my faith and trust in Him from the very beginning.

What I am saying is that it is possible to go to church, to read your Bible, to pray daily, to be involved in all sorts of church activities, and still not put your complete faith and trust in God. From my observations down through the years,

I am persuaded that many Christian people never get the blessing from God that He intended them to have because they do not really trust Him.

Paul found this to be true with people in the church at Corinth. In I Corinthians 3:1-2, he says, "I could not address you as spiritual, but as worldly—mere infants in Christ. I gave you milk, not solid food, for you were not yet ready for it." Do you see what he is saying? In essence, he said, "You never grew up (matured) as Christians. You still act like babies."

I don't want this to sound judgmental. I know many Christians who show by their lives every day that they trust in God for everything, but I am afraid there are many who do not, and it is my prayer that you will trust God completely from day one.

Why is this so important? It is the only way we can be what He expects us to be. The Bible is full of instructions for us. In Exodus 20:1-17, the second book in the Bible, we find the Ten Commandments, which is not a bad starting place. The balance of chapter twenty and chapters twenty-one and twenty-two go into great depth to explain the commandments. The first four commandments speak of our relationship with God, and the remaining six talk about our relationships with other people.

These are not old-fashioned rules that no longer apply to us. They are just as relevant today as they were when God gave them to Moses on Mount Sinai. As you read through them, stop and think of what the world would be like if people lived by these rules. There would be no crime, no spouses cheating on each other, no discord in families. The world would be a much better place if everyone would heed these commandments.

Next, turn over in your Bible to Matthew, the first book in the New Testament. The fifth, sixth, and seventh chapters are called The Sermon on the Mount. It is a sermon preached by Jesus, and it is basically a sermon about how to get along with people and how to obey God. Why not read those three chapters tomorrow morning, even if it means getting up fifteen minutes earlier than usual? Don't neglect reading these chapters. If you read carefully and heed what you read, it will make a significant difference in your life.

Also make a note to yourself to start reading in the book of Proverbs. There is a lot of wisdom contained in that book about your lifestyle.

Now let me get into some specifics. If you are really serious about becoming a Christian person who puts his or her entire trust in God, and one who wants to get as much as possible from his or her Christian walk, there are some things you need to do. We will cover several areas in the balance of this chapter and in the next few chapters.

FOUR KEYS TO BEING A HAPPY PRODUCTIVE CHRISTIAN

1) **Love God more than anyone or anything.** You should love God more than your wife, husband, children, parents, or anyone else. You should love God more than that new Mustang or Cadillac, or new home, or whatever it is in your life that seems so important. Mark 12:28-31 tells of a man who came to Jesus and asked Him, "Of all the commandments, which is the most important?" Jesus replied, "The most important one is this. Love the Lord your God with all your heart and with all your soul and with all your mind and with all your strength." He went on to say, "The second is this, Love your neighbor as yourself. There is no commandment greater than these."

God has to have first place in your life. That does not mean that you love your spouse or your children any less. But your desire to serve God must come first. What you will discover is that if you love God as He wants you to, you will become a better spouse, parent or young person, and that will bring a new dimension of happiness to those around you.

Notice that the text says, "Love your neighbor as yourself." If you are going to please God, you are going to love your family, and you are going to start putting first things first in your life. That includes learning to understand and appreciate the people around you and, most importantly, to be concerned for their spiritual well-being, no matter how different the color of their skin or their lifestyle is from your own. They need to have the same opportunity to know and to worship God that you do.

Several years ago a man who worked for me had some financial problems. He asked me for advice, so I went to his home and talked with him and his wife. I asked about their budget. He told me that on Friday afternoon, after they had both been paid, they would buy groceries. Then they would sit down and decide what bills absolutely had to be paid. Then he said, "With what is left, we decide how we can impress the most people."

I will give him credit for being one of the most honest people with financial problems that I have known. Most would not admit that they are trying to impress others, or that it was one of their high priorities. But it is true in many situations. People's egos get in the way of their common sense, and they spend what they don't have, or get involved in activities they shouldn't be involved in, because of what they perceive other people will think.

Things can become Gods that we worship, if we let them. Athletics, or athletes themselves, a fancy car, an expensive home—all can become our Gods if we are not careful. I know people who become tremendously upset because they envy the new house or the new car of a friend or neighbor. When you put God first in your life, *things* take on less importance, and your life will be much happier. I've tried it both ways, and I know I am right.

As a man, I found it difficult at first to say, "I love God." Somehow it didn't seem manly. Then I realized that if I was in a bad car accident and was lying in the roadway bleeding to death, and some one came along and provided the first aid that saved my life, I would owe that person a debt of eternal gratitude. The thought struck me that I would never be able to repay him for what he had done. I would "love him" for saving me. Then I found Romans 5:6-8, which says, "You see, at just the right time, when we were still powerless, Christ died for the ungodly. Very rarely will anyone die for a right-eous man, ...but God demonstrates his own love for us in this: While we were still sinners, Christ died for us."

Why shouldn't I love Him? He saved my life—not for just the time I am here on this earth, but for eternity.

Loving Him is more than just saying the words. Our actions show whether or not we really love Him. First John 3:17-18 says, "If anyone has material possessions and sees his brother in need but has no pity on him, how can the love of God be in him. Dear children, let us not love with words or tongue but with actions and in truth."

Now take a minute and turn to the next chapter in I John, chapter four and read from the eleventh verse through the end of the chapter.

So the first thing we need to do is to love God.

2) The second thing you may have to do is to **change your lifestyle**. Maybe you have already reached that conclusion. That means cleaning up your language or putting aside some old habits that are not good for your body or you. Your body is now the temple of the Holy Spirit (See 1 Corinthians 6:19). You may want to start with verse twelve. There is a lot to think about in those few verses.

If you have habits or relationships that are polluting your temple, it is time to stop. I know that is easier said than done, but I have never seen a situation where a Christian wanted to please God by cleaning up his act that God would not give him the strength through the Holy Spirit to do it. Second Thessalonians 2:13 says that the Spirit will sanctify (make holy) you. If you will allow the Holy Spirit to work in your life, He will help you get rid of the bad habits, the things that are displeasing to God. This takes a real commitment on your part, including daily Bible reading and prayer time. Losing weight, stopping smoking, or giving up alcoholic beverages, or swearing, or foul language, or breaking off a relationship that offends God—all are habits that the Holy Spirit can help us rid ourselves of if we will turn our lives over to God.

I had a young man in a church I pastored who came forward one Sunday to make his profession of faith and to ask to be baptized. I found out he was living with his girlfriend. I told him I could not baptize him unless that relationship was resolved in marriage or their living apart. Four weeks later he was back to be baptized. She had moved out. When he started talking to God about the relationship, he realized that this was not what either of them really wanted for the rest of their lives. I was afraid we might not see her again, but in just a few weeks she came back to church, and at the invitation time in the service, she asked to be baptized. They have since gone in separate directions. He is a very active member of that same church and has led others to the Lord.

Just a few years ago I sat at the bedside of a very dear friend. He was dying from lung cancer. He had been a heavy cigarette smoker. I saw the pain and agony that he went through and the trauma that his family suffered seeing him die. I thought to myself, *We do so many things to harm ourselves and others. We desecrate our bodies with our bad habits. We spend money we don't have. We say things without thinking. When will we ever learn?*

God doesn't want us to live our lives with a lot of "You can't do this" and "You can't do that" hanging over us. In no way is He trying to take the fun out of life. He wants us to live pure, clean lives so we can enjoy our life more, and so we don't cause ourselves and those around us any unnecessary grief.

3) Third, ***we need to have complete faith and trust in God*** to provide for all of our needs. We have already covered this in detail, so we won't spend more time on that subject here. Suffice it to say that those who learn early on to trust God and put all their faith in Him are much better off than those who are cocky enough to think they can handle most everything on their own.

4) One of the things we cannot ignore, if we are to be true servants of God, is that process of continually learning more about what God has to say to us. There are people who profess to be Christians, but they never open their Bibles from one Sunday to the next, and oftentimes not even on Sunday. ***Studying God's Word*** is vital to our relationship to Him. He tells us in 2 Timothy 2:15, "Do your best (study) to present yourself to God as one approved, a workman who does not need to be ashamed and who correctly handles the word of truth." How is it possible to correctly handle the Word of Truth if we don't know what it says?

Let me encourage you to start some new habits right now. Sit down and think about your daily schedule and your personal habits. If you don't mind getting up in the morning, start getting up just fifteen minutes earlier than you have been used to. If you are a night person who likes to stay up late, you may want to choose a time period later in the day. The point is to pick a time each day and stick to it. Give yourself at least fifteen to twenty minutes each day to communicate with God.

Find a quiet place where you won't be disturbed. Shut the door or find a way to be by yourself and let your family know that this is your quiet time. Some people will tell you to pray first, others to study the Bible first. Do whichever works best for you. Some who don't get up too easily will find it hard to get awake if they start out in prayer. Shutting their eyes to pray may put them right back to sleep. I like to pray first, and while I am praying, I ask God to help me understand what I read when I do my Bible study.

The important thing is to faithfully have a time each day to pray and to read God's Word. I walk three miles every morning. I do fifteen minutes of floor exercises and then go walking. While I am walking I pray. Then when I get home, I do my Bible study. I spend more than fifteen or twenty minutes each day, but I am at an age where I don't have to be at work at 8:00 or 8:30 every morning. Start with fifteen or twenty minutes. Use it wisely, and you will be well on your way to establishing a good habit.

What are you going to study? Well, for the next few weeks you have your work cut out for you right here. I hope you are studying this book each day and will continue to study it until you have completed it.

Next, I suggest that you read through your Bible. It will take a while. But if you went to the library and borrowed a book, or if you bought a book at the bookstore, you would read it from front to back simply because it makes more sense to do it that way—unless you are like my wife, who always reads the last four or five pages first. She wants to know how it is going to come out before she spends time reading the whole book.

You will find some places a little difficult, where there are several pages of genealogy, but you will also find a lot of exciting and informative stories about those who lived in Old Testament times and those who lived during and shortly after Christ was here on earth. Read it front to back. Set up a plan to read a certain number of pages each day.

The first time I read it through, I looked to see how many pages my Bible had and divided that by 350. It worked out to four pages a day, which meant that if I was faithful to my plan, I could read the entire Bible in a year. Down through the years I have read the Bible through several times in different translations, and I learn many new things each time I do it.

There are plans where you read from both the Old and New Testaments each day, or plans where you skip around, but whatever the plan, read the entire Bible in a year. The first time, let me encourage you to read from front to back, just as you would any other book.

Along with this, do yourself a favor. Memorize the books of the Bible in sequence. I heard those groans. "I don't memorize well." "I'm too old to memorize." "I have too much stuff to memorize at school." There are dozens of excuses, but there isn't one good excuse.

Most Bible study teachers have learned not to call on class members to read a Scripture without warning them in advance, but it does occasionally happen. It could be a moment of embarrassment for you to be called on and not know where the passage is. In most churches the pastor will encourage people to follow him in their own Bible as he reads the Scripture passage aloud. If you have to look in the Table of Contents to find where the book is, and then fumble around finding it, you will still be looking when everyone else is through reading. Memorizing the books of the Bible is not an awesome task. Do five books a day, then the next day, do the first five again and add five more. In two weeks you will be able to name all the books in the Bible in their proper order. You will always benefit from this knowledge. It will give you great satisfaction, and it will be an immense help to you through the years.

You will also want to start memorizing some of the Scriptures you read that are especially meaningful to you. You never know when you might be in a situation where being able to quote a Scripture you have memorized will be extremely helpful to you. It all starts with reading His Word faithfully and studying it enough to understand what God is saying to you.

If you purchased a Study Bible, be sure to read the notes as you read the passage. Take time to look up some of the references. You may wish to read the passage straight through one morning and then study the notes and references the next morning. As you come to appreciate God's Word more and more, you will experience a growing desire to learn the details of what you read. At that point, you may want to talk with the religious bookstore in your neighborhood about a laymen's commentary. Depending on the publisher, this can be one or more books that help you to study the Bible by explaining in more detail what each passage means.

So study faithfully and—who knows?—in a couple years you may desire to teach the Bible to others. There is no better way to learn than to have the opportunity to teach. In our next chapter we will continue with thoughts on the other part of our quiet time, prayer.

CHAPTER 7

Make It a Matter of Prayer

After we take time to read His Word each day, I can hear the next question. "What am I going to pray about?" You may be thinking, *I can't think of enough things to pray about to pray for five or ten minutes.* And that may be true if you pray only for yourself and your immediate family. Get out of that habit right now. There is nothing wrong with praying about your needs and those of your family, but don't make those the only subjects of your prayers.

Charles Swindoll, my favorite radio pastor and President of the Dallas Theological Seminary, says in his book The Bride that the primary purpose of worship is to glorify God.[1] In fact, the primary purpose of our lives as Christians is to glorify God. If what I do does not glorify Him, then I shouldn't do it. In other words, if my actions or words do not glorify Him but instead bring disrepute to His name, then they are wrong.

Let's apply that to our prayer life. If I spend my time praying for things for myself, or for asking God to get even with people for something they did to me, that is not going to glorify God. So I need to ask before I pray, "Is this going to glorify God if I pray for it?" Conversely, if I am praying for my pastor or for our church to be what God wants it to be, that is going to glorify Him. If I pray for the welfare of our missionaries, or that God will guide the doctors and nurses as they care for the health of someone seriously ill, that will glorify God.

If I pray that our country will turn to God and that our leaders will use godly principles in governing us, or that the person who is not a Christian that I met and talked to the other day will accept Him as their Savior—that will glorify God.

These are just a few examples of things you can pray for in a way that will please God. First, you should express your thanks to Him for being who He is and what He has done in your life. Thank Him that you have come to know Him. Thank Him for forgiving your sins and making you one of His children. Thank Him for the country you live in and the freedom you enjoy. Praise Him for your parents and grandparents and others who have been positive influences in your life. Some mornings, I spend my entire prayer time thanking God. Try it. It will make you stop and appreciate things you often take for granted, and help you to realize that God is the Creator and Owner of all you possess, and He is worthy of all of your praise.

In your church or Sunday school class, there will always be a list of people who need to be prayed for. Some churches and classes prepare the list in written form for Wednesday night prayer meeting or another time of prayer in the church. Bring this list home with you and put it in your Bible so it will be handy when you pray each morning.

You may be asking why it is necessary to pray so regularly. Why shouldn't I just pray when I have a need? The Bible tells us it is important to have fellowship with God regularly. God has always been interested in man. The Bible says God created man in His own image. And down through the centuries, God has had a close association with man. What great world leader wants to be with you and me? God does.

He is continually encouraging us to pray to Him. He has always made every effort to communicate with man.

In the first five books of the Bible, there are 187 chapters. In 139 of these chapters, we find God approaching man. He talks with Adam in the garden. He converses with Cain about his anger. Noah, Abraham, and Moses all had conversations with God. He wants us to be near Him.

In Jeremiah 29:10-14, God tells Jeremiah that when the seventy-year Captivity in Babylon is over, God will prosper the people as they return home. Verse twelve says, "Then you will call upon me and come and pray to me and I will listen to you." Read all of these verses and see God's promises to His people as they communicate with Him.

The first thing we see as we move to the New Testament is God communicating with man once again by sending His Son, Jesus Christ, to teach and heal and then to give His life for our sins. (See Philippians 2:6-8.)

In James 4:8, it tells us to "come near to God and He will come near to you." I don't know how He does it. I just know He is all powerful. He hears us when we pray and encourages us to have fellowship with Him. I have seen too many prayers answered of my own and others to not believe God hears and responds.

God not only encourages us to pray to Him, He commands us to pray. Let's look at several verses. They speak for themselves:

Jeremiah 33:3—"Call to me and I will answer you, and tell you great and unsearchable things you do not know."

Isaiah 55:6—"Seek the Lord while he may be found, call on Him while He is near."

Psalm 50:15—"Call upon me in the day of trouble; I will deliver you, and you will honor me."

Matthew 7:7—"Ask and it will be given to you; seek and you will find; knock and the door will be opened to you."

Luke 18:1—"Then Jesus told his disciples a parable to show them that they should always pray and not give up."

Read verses 2-8 to see the parable Jesus told illustrating the fact that we should pray and not give up.

Colossians 4:2—"Devote yourselves to prayer, being watchful and thankful."

1 Timothy 2:1—"I urge then, first of all, that requests, prayers, intercession and thanksgiving be made for everyone."

Samuel thought it was a sin not to pray. "As for me, far be it from me that I should sin against the Lord by failing to pray for you." (1 Samuel 12:23).

But people do fail to pray. Surveys of pastors and laypeople alike indicate that many Christians don't pray from one Sunday to the next. Many who do pray, pray less than five minutes a day. In many churches the time devoted to prayer becomes less and less. Worship without prayer is meaningless.

Preacher Hallock, a great prayer warrior, said, "When we become thankless, we become sinners against God." Learn to thank Him. Learn to be a prayer warrior yourself.

Earlier we studied the Holy Spirit. We talked about how He indwells in us and that we are the temple in which He lives. When our prayer life drops off, we cut off the power between God and the Holy Spirit in us. It is like throwing the breaker switch at the electric box. We shut down God's power in our lives.

God promises us that even if we don't know what to pray, the Holy Spirit will help us. Romans 8:26-27 says, "In the same way, the Spirit helps us in our weakness. We do not know what we ought to pray for, but the Spirit himself intercedes for us with groans that words cannot express. And he who searches our hearts knows the mind of the Spirit, because the Spirit intercedes for the saints in accordance with God's will."

The Bible has a lot to say about prayer. We cannot cover it all here, but you remember we talked earlier about the features in your Bible. One very important part of your Bible is the concordance. It is in the back of your Bible and looks something like a dictionary. It is divided alphabetically into words that appear frequently in the Bible and lists where they can be found. It also gives part of the sentence in which they appear so it is easier to locate a particular verse you may be looking for. Take time now to look up the word pray in the concordance in your Bible.

There will undoubtedly be more than one word related to prayer. *Pray, prayed, prayer, prayers, praying, prays,* may appear, one after the other. Look under pray for example and you will see several times that pray is used in the Bible. These words are listed in the order they appear in the Bible with the Old Testament references first, followed by the New Testament ones. The book the reference is in is listed in an abbreviated form, then come the chapter and verse, and then a part of the sentence in which the word is used.

You will probably find in your concordance some listings in Matthew (it may be abbreviated Mt). Now open your Bible to Matthew the sixth chapter and let's look at verses 5-15. If your Bible is a red letter Bible, you will find all of Christ's sayings in red ink. And you will note that almost all of chapters five, six, and seven are in red. This is known as the Sermon on the Mount. Jesus is teaching His disciples, and it is a presentation of righteous living for those who are a part of God's family. Note that several verses are devoted to prayer. In 6:5, Jesus starts by telling the disciples how not to pray. He says not to stand out where everyone can see you, making your praying obvious. Secret yourself in a quiet place and don't just "babble" on and on.

Then in verse nine Jesus gives you a pattern to show you how to pray. He says, "This, then, is how you should pray." This is not a suggestion to just repeat this exact prayer over and over again. The pattern is what is important.

He begins by praising God and expressing adoration of Him. Then He says that He is subject to God's will, and that He will do His best to do what God wants Him to do in every phase of His life. Then He submits His requests or petitions to God. These are the things Christ is concerned about. These are the people He is praying for today. This is the work of God's kingdom that He is interested in.

Then He tells us to ask for forgiveness for our sins—not just a broad brushed plea for forgiveness. When you pray, this should be a time to mention some specific things that you know you are doing wrong. Recounting them before God will help you to resolve to break these bad habits, or help make you aware of what you need to do to make amends.

If you have the New International Version, the Revised Standard Version, or some of the other newer translations, you will note that a part of what we know as The Lord's Prayer is missing. If you have said this prayer or heard it sung, it finishes with: "For Thine is the kingdom and the power, and the glory, for ever, Amen." This part was not in the early manuscripts, but was added later and included in the King James translation. Because it was not in the early manuscripts, it was deleted from the newer translations. But this does not mean that praising God for His goodness is not an appropriate way to conclude your prayers. Quite the opposite is true. Glorifying God at the beginning and at the end of your prayers is quite appropriate.

Don't quit reading at the end of the model prayer. The next two verses speak about our forgiveness of others. When we pray for forgiveness of our own sins, we need to be sure we have forgiven others who have hurt or harmed us in any way—a very important step to learn in our Christian growth.

Prayer doesn't stop with a few minutes each morning to ask God to bless us and our family, or even to spend fifteen or twenty minutes pouring out our heart to Him. Prayer is one of the vital ways that we communicate with God. We also communicate by reading His word, the Bible; and by having the Holy Spirit in our lives.

Prayer is the way we approach God. E.F. Hallock was the pastor for many years at the First Baptist Church in Norman, Oklahoma, where the University of Oklahoma is located. I heard him preach many years ago. He came to our church one time and devoted an entire week of sermons to prayer. He also wrote a book called *Always in Prayer*. I would recommend that you read his book if you can find it in your church library. One of the things he says is that prayer is the way we approach God. James 4:8 says, "Draw nigh to God." Prayer is the way we do that.

Now, if we love God more than anyone else, which is what we should do, then He should be our best friend. You don't treat your best friends as though they didn't exist, or that you are bored to be in their company. You don't designate a limited amount of time each day to spend with your best friend and then ignore him the rest of the day. You treat best friends with respect. You praise them for being kind to you. You try to make your time with them worthwhile and meaningful. Sometimes you just like to have them near even though nothing is said, but their presence is gratifying to you. If Christ is not your best friend, then you need to start working on it. He should be. The only way He can be your best friend is for you to know Him well. That comes by close association—talking with Him several times a day and reading His Word regularly.

It is hard to ask people for help if you don't know them well, and for those people who only call on God when they are in trouble, it must be very difficult to have to explain their way into God's presence. Look at Psalm 86:1-4. David says in verse two, "I am devoted to you." Are you devoted to God? Learn to know Him so that your devotion will grow. Now before we move on, read the rest of the Psalm 86. There is a lot to think about there.

This is how your time with God should be. You shouldn't ignore Him for several days and then, when you get in a bind, pray up a storm for a day or two and then forget Him again as soon as that problem is resolved.

Your time with Him should be exciting and important to you. Prayer time is not a boring time. You are in God's presence, and you should be anxious to share with Him what is on your mind. You should also spend some time in quiet contemplation so that He can speak to you.

Prayer time shouldn't be structured so that you start every morning at 6:35 and quit at 6:47, and that's it for the day. Your prayer time shouldn't be limited to the few minutes each day in your quiet place. Some of your most meaningful prayer times may come at work or school or driving down the freeway. Perhaps a fellow worker, student, or client drops by your desk or confronts you in the hall and shares a problem that is on their heart. Maybe it is an illness of a loved one, a broken relationship, or a move they are suddenly facing. Don't wait until tomorrow morning at 6:35 to pray for them. If they are a Christian, or you feel they would appreciate a time of prayer, get by yourselves in a private office or a corner of the hallway and pray with them about their concern right then. You may not know the person you are praying for, but some of the most meaningful prayers come from the lips of strangers.

A thought comes to you driving down the freeway. It is something you need to pray about. I don't recommend shutting your eyes for this prayer, but God will hear your prayer. It is very possible that the Holy Spirit may have initiated the thought to begin with.

Show respect to God as you pray. Praise Him for being close to you and providing for you. It is all right to tell Him you don't understand why a certain thing happened the way that it did, as long as you assure Him that you want His will to be done. You will not always understand why some things happen, and we will talk more about that in chapter 8. Look at

Isaiah 55:8 for a moment. God is saying to us that He knows what is ultimately best for us. He wants us to tell Him how we feel, but it should always be His will we are subject to.

Sometimes you may want to get away where it is quiet and think about all the good things God has done for you. The longer you are a Christian, the more you should see that things in your life are different than they used to be. If your life has not changed as the result of being a Christian, there is something wrong. Look for the differences and praise God for them.

In 1 Thessalonians 5:17, it says we are to "pray continually" or "without ceasing." This does not mean that you should never do anything but pray. It does mean that as you go through the day, you should be wise enough to stop and pray when you sense the need to, or when a situation arises that could use your prayers.

When our daughter was seriously ill with cancer, we knew that God heard our prayers. What we did not know at the time was that many people who we did not know personally, were praying for her.

Several years later, a friend of mine called and asked if I would help a secretary in his office with some insurance papers concerning her husband's death. After we had finished the paper work, she asked how Helen was doing. I was surprised because I didn't even know she knew Helen. This was the first time she and I had ever had more conversation than just a "Hello. He's in his office" type of exchange.

As we talked about Helen, she said, "You know the night the doctors told you Helen would not live through the night? I heard about that from Luke [her boss]. When I got home from work, I was so upset about that little girl being so sick, I couldn't go to sleep, even though I had never met her. So I knelt down by my bed and prayed all night that God would heal her."

James 5:15-16 says, "And the prayer offered **in faith** will make the sick person well; the Lord will raise him up. If he has sinned, he will be forgiven. Therefore confess your sins to each other and pray for each other so that you may be healed. The prayer of a righteous man is powerful and effective."(The boldface of "in faith" is mine.) God cannot work in our lives if we don't have faith. His will must be done. But we understand that, if we have faith.

The amount of time that many Christian people actually spend in prayer is shameful. All across the land, prayer meetings have disappeared from the schedule of many churches, or the time for prayer is very limited. Some Christian people admittedly spend less than five minutes a day in prayer. I would encourage you to be a force in your church to return to the Scripture in 2 Chronicles 7:14 that says, "If my people, who are called by my name, will humble themselves and pray and seek my face and turn from their wicked ways, then will I hear from heaven and will forgive their sin and will heal their land."

In recent years, many churches have started prayer rooms where members sign up to spend an hour each week praying for their church, for missionaries from their denomination, and for other needs. Find out if your church has a prayer room. I'm sure there will be a spot on the calendar for you. If your church doesn't have one, it might be a project for you to initiate.

We live in a country and in a time where we need to return to prayer and humble ourselves so that God can heal our nation and its people. Prayer changes things, and it can start with you.

Endnotes

1 Swindoll, *The Bride* (Zondervan, 1994), p. 19.

CHAPTER 8

Why Do Christians Sometimes Suffer?

God's people are not immune to suffering. This will probably not come as a shock to you. Christians do sometimes suffer, and we need to talk about it. Christians get sick, sometimes with incurable diseases. Occasionally they lose their jobs. They have financial setbacks, possibly losing almost all they own. Or they may have someone in their family whom they love who goes through a time of trauma. All Christians go through pain and suffering at some time in their lives, probably more than once.

One thing I have noticed through the years is that quite often a new Christian runs into some difficulty, such as an illness or a problem with their job. It is very likely that the devil is putting up roadblocks or trying to discourage those who have recently made a commitment to God. Read 1 Peter 5:8. I believe that we need to look at the problem of why Christian people suffer and give some insight on how to deal with pain and suffering.

My wife and I have some friends from a church where we used to live that have had tragedy strike their family multiple times. They have always been a strong church-going family. The wife taught a Bible study group for ladies on a weekday morning. Her husband taught Bible study on Sundays.

Several years ago, while they were doing a favor for someone else, their car was struck by a drunk driver, and their one-year-old baby son was killed. The mother was in the hospital for the better part of a year. The husband lost his job because he was taking a lot of time off to care for his wife. A few years later, another son was diagnosed with brain cancer and spent several years undergoing costly treatment. Then the father had a heart attack and died. Next, just a short time later, the oldest son was killed in a car accident. Then the son with cancer died.

When things stack up like this, many people would start to question, "Why does God let this happen? or "Why is God doing this to us?"

There have been several books written on the subject. Two of the better ones, in my opinion, are *When God Doesn't Make Sense* by James Dobson, and *Why Us? When Bad Things Happen to God's People* by Warren Wiersbe. You may want to purchase one of these for an in-depth study on this subject. But for the next few pages we will talk about this subject in a brief fashion.

Let's go back to our first statement. God's people are not immune to suffering. It has never been any different. When we look at the Old Testament, God's early history of His people, we see people suffering. Adam and Eve, the first couple, had a son who killed his brother. Adam and Eve had to have suffered when this happened.

Joseph was the favorite son of his father. He was given the nicest clothes and evidently didn't have to spend the time his brothers did taking care of the flocks. Then suddenly he was sold into slavery by his brothers. He was hustled off to Egypt and thrown into prison because he was falsely accused. For years his father thought he was dead. (See Genesis 39.)

Moses killed a man and had to hide in the desert for forty years, tending his father-in-law's herds—probably not what he would like to have done all those years if he had been given a choice. Then God made him a tour guide for two to three million people.[1] His job was to lead the Israelite nation out of captivity in Egypt. Can you imagine trying to please a couple of million people where food and water were almost nonexistent and where there were no Holiday Inns within walking distance. The book of Exodus tells this exciting story of God's provision in the midst of their difficulties.

My point is that God's people are not made an exception when it comes to suffering. Quite the opposite is true. The Bible says that there will be suffering, and that these times are opportunities for growth. Sometimes you may have to face the pain and agony of watching a loved one suffer with cancer or Alzheimer's disease. Or you may have the worry that comes with knowing there is more month left than there is money, and then the boss says he is downsizing and is going to have to let you go.

When these things happen, it is almost a natural instinct to cry out to God, "Why are you letting this happen to me?" I understand that even atheists have been known to cry out in this way. We don't like pain. We don't want to hurt, and we pray that God will keep pain and suffering out of our lives.

Let me say at this point that no one I know has all the answers to the question of why Christians suffer. I would say to beware of the person who claims to have all the answers. There are people out there who will draw you in by saying, "Name it and claim it." "If you know the right things to say, you can ask Jesus for anything and it will be yours." That is not true. God isn't running a candy store and handing out free coupons. You will never know all the reasons why Christian people suffer, but you probably already know that God doesn't give you a life of ease and plenty just because you ask for it. You will have your share of suffering as you go through the rest of your life here. So let's look at some of the answers to why Christians suffer.

Maybe we should start by saying God's perspective is completely different than ours. He created everything. He owns it all. He gives us what we need, not necessarily what we want. He knows how He would like for us to use what He gives us and what He wants us to be. Unfortunately for some of us, He gives us the freedom to choose, and we don't always make the right choices. God lets us make up our own minds about choosing Him, obeying Him, and serving Him. And that is where a lot of the trouble starts.

First of all, we may be in competition with some other Christians who want the same thing. Let's say the star forward on Junction City's basketball team is a Christian. The center of Capital City's basketball team is also a Christian. They meet for the state championship, and both players pray earnestly that their team will be the new state champion. When one of them loses, he says, "God didn't answer my prayers." Just because both chose to be Christians, both expect God to be on their side. Personally I think God leaves basketball championships, our golf game, and many other things that we do and pray for to our own abilities, unless He sees an opportunity for us to grow as a Christian through the experience.

For example, He might be concerned about our pride, and He realizes that we need some losses in our life so we will put that pride away. Or He knows that the promotion we have been praying for will keep us from getting involved in a project He has planned for us, and so He delays that promotion for a while.

We may also make bad choices that God can't be responsible for. If we smoke two packs of cigarettes a day or chew snuff, we shouldn't blame God for the consequences of lung or lip cancer. If we drink alcoholic beverages and get cancer of the liver or become an alcoholic, that is not God's fault. If we spend more money than we make and carry large balances on our credit cards, we are going to get into financial trouble, and God is not to blame for that. When we eat all kinds of junk food and carry forty or fifty pounds of excess weight around, God can't be responsible for our heart attack. If we decide an affair outside of marriage is the answer to our unhappiness, then the consequences, which are guaranteed to happen, are not God's fault. That is sin in our life, and God can't be blamed because we make the wrong choices.

Do you see what I am saying? God gave us the freedom to choose what we will do with our life. It goes further than choosing whether or not we will be a Christian. Many times, bad choices are made. Sometimes our lifetime habits and some of our everyday decisions are settled in our mind without seriously considering what God would have us do. We need to look at the consequences that will result from our actions. Quite often, this will lead us to the conclusion that we need to change the way we are living, or to get rid of the bad habits.

We all sin. Romans 3:10 says, "There is none righteous, not even one." We have to be wise enough to realize when we have sinned. It is not a time to question God or to blame Him for the results. It is a time to humble ourselves, get down on our knees, and ask God's forgiveness, and then get up from our knees determined to not make that mistake again. Even if it is a lifetime habit, God will forgive us and give us the strength to break the habit if we will pray and keep on praying with the faith that He does answer our prayers.

However, we need to make it clear that not everything that happens to us is our fault. There is no Bible scholar, no book, no crystal ball that will explain why we sometimes suffer through no fault of our own.

For example, the book of Job in the Bible tells of a man who lost almost all he had because Satan wanted to prove to God that Job was a good man only because he had been blessed by God. The trial that came upon Job was not his fault. He had been abundantly blessed by God, and now Satan was taking it away. Unfortunately for Job, some of his friends proved to be very poor friends. They encouraged him to blame God and himself for all his problems. They may have been envious of Job when he was well-to-do and had a successful family, and now they could turn that envy on him in his time of trouble. They didn't understand that the devil was at work in their world to try to discourage a man like Job, who wanted to honor and serve God.

That is just as true today. Many of those we would consider our friends seem to get satisfaction out of seeing us struggle when the tough times hit, and just at a time when we need encouragement.

Quite often, Christian people blame themselves needlessly, which only adds to their problems. Or they blame God. In truth, it may be Satan working on them, or it may just be the circumstances of this life in a fallen world.

The key to this kind of situation in your life is not to start thinking that somehow you must be to blame, or to feel that God has somehow lost control. As Dr. Dobson says in his book *When God Doesn't Make Sense.* "It is not your responsibility to explain what God is doing with your life. He has not provided enough information to figure it out. Instead, you are asked to turn loose and let God be God. Therein lies the secret to the 'peace that transcends understanding.'"[2] Remember our talk about faith in the first chapter? When you are hurting and there doesn't seem to be a logical reason for it, it is a good time to exercise your faith and trust that God knows you are hurting, and in His time it will be worked out.

The last half of John 16:33 says it very well. "In this world you will have trouble. But take heart! I have overcome the world." God is all-powerful. He knows what is going on in our lives. He is in control.

It may be that there is something God wants us to learn, and the only way we can learn is for Him to get our attention.

We have to learn to trust Him no matter what is happening in our lives. In Isaiah 55:8, God says, "For my thoughts are not your thoughts, neither are your ways my ways." Don't always feel that there has to be an explanation or a reason that is plain to us. Learn to ask, "What does God want me to learn from this experience?" rather than, "Why are you letting this happen to me?"

In 1985, my wife and I sold our two real estate offices and retired in the Hill Country of Texas. We built a beautiful home on the lake with a double boathouse and all of the trimmings. Our retirement income was coming from interest payments on notes we held on land we had sold and from dividends on Savings and Loan and bank stocks. Our advisors had said these investments were the safest place we could put our money.

Shortly after our retirement, the Congress passed a law allowing Savings and Loan institutions to invest in just about anything they wanted to. And this is what most of them did. The result was a catastrophe. Within a couple of years, many of the Savings and Loans went broke. The land they held as collateral on loans they had made was turned over to the Resolution Trust Corporation, a government entity. The Resolution Trust immediately put this land on the market at bargain basement prices. Soon the people we had sold land to, who were paying us interest, called and said, "We can buy land from the RTC for a fraction of what we owe you. So we are going to quit paying on our notes to you." And they did. In six months, our retirement income had dried up. We had the land back with taxes to pay on it and a bunch of worthless Savings and Loan stock certificates. So at retirement age, we had to put our "dream home" up for sale and go back to work. I started blaming God and then myself.

Several years earlier, I had tried to write a book on selling. I had been a salesman or a sales manager almost all of my life. I started selling magazines door to door at age eight. I sold clothes to earn my way through college. Then I sold life insurance and managed life insurance sales offices for over twenty years before going into real estate sales.

Now we were without income, and I decided to get out the manuscript on my sales book and polish it up in hopes I could sell it. I thought maybe that would help us out of our financial crisis. I pulled it up on my computer and started reading through it. What a revelation. It was one big brag book. I did this. I did that. Look at me, how good I am. And then it hit me. God was using this experience of losing our retirement income to point out to me that although I had been a Christian for fifty years, I had never lost my pride in my possessions or my dependence on myself instead of trusting in Him. I had never really turned it all over to Him. It was late in life to have to learn a lesson like this, but I feel that it has changed my life dramatically.

Six years later, we were able to go to Canada as volunteers to work at the Canadian Southern Baptist Seminary. We worked there for two years, trusting in God to provide, and He did. We were able to spend those two years raising funds, taking care of flower beds, managing student housing, cooking and serving meals—trying to help wherever we saw that help was needed.

Just before we left Texas to go to Canada, our church ordained me to the ministry, which was completely unexpected. As a result, I was able to pastor a small church in Calgary without having to depend on the church for a salary.

God knew what He was doing and what He wanted me to do. He just had to get my attention before it could come about. He knew how to take care of us. Before we left Texas, we were told we could only get a one-year work permit in Canada. When we arrived at the Canadian border, the lady we had corresponded with had taken the day off. I was afraid we would have problems as a result of having to deal with someone who knew nothing about us. Wrong! The young lady who waited on us got out our file and asked us how long we wanted our permit for. I told her we would like a two-year permit, and that was the way she typed it up.

We didn't know what we would do for health insurance while we were there, so the day after we arrived, we went to the province health insurance office. The lady there asked us how long our work permit was for. I told her "two years." She replied, "That's good. With a two-year permit, we can give you health coverage, and because you are age sixty-five, it will be free." Do you think God doesn't know how to take care of us?

Stop and think about it. Don't most of the good things in life come from trials? New medicines come from years of research in the laboratory. A college diploma comes from years of discipline and study. The Tiger Woods and Troy Aikmans come from years of practice and discipline. The Billy Grahams come from the discipline of study and practice and long hours of prayer.

In *Why Us?* Warren Wiersbe says, "God never promised to pamper and shelter His people. He did promise to strengthen us for the battle and helps us to win the victory. 'Do not pray for easy lives,' said Phillips Brooks. 'Pray for powers equal to the tasks.'" [3]

I want you to pay particular attention to this paragraph because I want to talk for a moment about a very misused verse in the Bible. Romans 8:28 says, "Everything works together for good," and that is where a lot of people who quote this verse stop. They meet someone who is hurting from a serious illness or a death in the family or some other tragedy, and they think they are going to cheer that person up by saying, "Everything works together for good."

In that sense of the word, everything does not work together for good. There are many times that things happen where it would be difficult to find any good that has come out of the incident. There are tragic accidents, illness, floods, fires and other disasters where it is difficult to see any good. Is the

Bible wrong? No! There is more to that verse that needs to be quoted if you are going to use it. It says, "Everything works together for good for those who love the Lord and are called according to His purpose." If we love the Lord and have turned over our lives to Him in complete surrender, He can use even the bad things that happen to us to work some good. Let me illustrate.

When our daughter Helen was diagnosed with cancer, it was hard to see where anything good could come from a five-year-old having what was considered to be a terminal illness. But because of the love of God, today, forty years later, we can look back and count at least six people who came to know the Lord as a direct result of her illness and healing.

Because I have used her healing as a topic for sermons in many churches, it is impossible to measure the impact that Helen's illness and healing has had.

The same is true with our loss of our retirement income. Had that income continued, I would have probably stayed fat, dumb and happy, spending all of my days playing golf and riding our boat. You probably are thinking, "That doesn't sound too bad to me," but it doesn't get God's work done that He would like for us to participate in. I would never have been ordained or pastored a church. I know of twenty-five people I have led to the Lord that I wouldn't even have met if our lives hadn't changed quite dramatically.

God will use the bad things that happen to us to work good, because "everything works together for good, for those who love the Lord and are called according to His purpose."

If God was fair in His dealings with us, we would be in misery most of the time because all of us deserve a lot more punishment than what we receive. I do things every day that God could punish me for if He were only interested in being fair. But because He loves you and me, He blesses a lot more than He punishes.

We are going to hurt sometimes. That's life on this earth. For Christian or non-Christian alike, there will be times when we think the world is falling in on us, when our own illness or that of someone we love brings them close to death, or some other problem almost seems to overwhelm us. Those are the times when we must be very careful not to indulge in self-pity. It is easy to blame God and to feel sorry for ourselves. That only makes matters worse. Self-pity is unadulterated selfishness. If you catch yourself self-indulging, get out and do something for somebody else. Go visit in the nursing home. Find a needy family in your community. Find out what their needs are and gather some clothing or food to take to them. Call your church and ask for the names of some shut-ins you can visit. Take a devotional book with you and read to them, or pray with them. Take them for a walk if they are able. You will soon find that your problems are not so bad after all.

God wants us to have faith in Him. He wants us to trust Him. We can use the trials that come our way in life to feel sorry for ourselves, or we can use them to show God how strong our faith and trust in Him is.

Read Daniel 3 and look at the faith of Shadrach, Meshach, and Abednego. That is the kind of faith God will honor, and it is the kind of faith that will glorify His name.

Why do Christians suffer? I don't believe God causes many of these things to happen. But I do believe He will use them to His honor and glory if we will respond in faith and trust. Be assured that God is there with you when you face the problems of life, and He will support you.

It is very important for us to remember that our life on this earth is just a small moment out of eternity. In a short period of time, eternally speaking, no matter what has happened to us or to our loved ones here on this earth, we will be together for eternity. There will be no more pain or sorrow, unhappiness, disappointment or worry, if we trust in Christ as our Savior. We also know that those who have gone before are finished with their pain and suffering, and they are with a

God who is much, much greater and more powerful than our minds can conceive.

Psalm 86 is a psalm you need to read right now. It is a prayer from David that expresses very beautifully what a great and awesome God we have.

To conclude this chapter, I have written a poem to express in my own way what I feel our attitude should be about the suffering of Christian people.

> When Jesus was hung on Calvary's tree
> He didn't complain, or try to break free..
> He didn't blame God for the plight He was in
> He was willing to die there because of my sin.
>
> He didn't curse at me or at you—
> He prayed, "Forgive them, they know not what they do."
> He wasn't there as punishment for anything He'd done;
> He was there in obedience as God's only son.
>
> So why do we blame God when something goes wrong?
> Why don't we keep a faith that is loyal and strong?
> Why can't we realize, pain is a part of this life;
> We live in a world where there will always be strife?
>
> Joseph and Moses and Job suffered too;
> But God loved them all, just as He loves you.
> And because Christ suffered, and rose to live again;
> Someday we'll be in heaven where there's no pain or sin.

Endnotes

1 *Ryrie Study Bible; New International Version* (Moody Press,1986) p. 186.

2 Dobson, *When God Doesn't Make Sense* (Tyndale House 1993) p. 167

3 Wiersbe, *Why Us?* (Revell, 1984), p. 61.

CHAPTER 9

Baptism and the Lord's Supper

This is an area in which you will find quite a bit of difference from one denomination to another. If you talked with
members of any denomination, they would justify what they
believe about the ordinances of the church and probably use
some Scriptures to back them up.

Over the past two thousand years, however, many denominations have slipped away from what the Bible tells us to do
because of expediency or because what they believe was a
misunderstanding of what the Scripture really says. A lot of
the difference is plainly in the interpretation of what the
Scripture says. As Southern Baptists, we have tried very diligently to follow closely what we believe the Scriptures tell us
about the ordinances.

I am not going to attempt to compare what Southern
Baptists believe with what all the other denominations practice. I will mention practices of some churches to help you
better understand, but mainly I will talk about the two ordinances practiced by Southern Baptists and refer you to several

Scriptures to justify our adherence to those two ordinances and our manner of observing them.

You have heard the word "ordinance" before. City governments have ordinances that regulate the way that residents and visitors of that community behave. City councils may pass new "ordinances" as they see the need for them.

The dictionary says an ordinance is an "authoritative rule," or a "religious rite or ceremony," a "law or command of God." Some churches refer to ordinances as "sacraments" because they believe they are related to our salvation.

Southern Baptists have two "commands of God" we feel are important practices that should be observed on a regular basis in our church: baptism, and the Lord's Supper. Each local church's autonomy (we'll talk about that word in chapter 11) makes it possible for two churches in the same community to set their own times and manners for observing these ordinances. So you will no doubt see some differences between various Baptist churches as to when these ordinances are practiced and how they are carried out, but there are some fundamentals that should be observed by all Southern Baptist churches.

Let's take the ordinances one at a time and get a clear understanding of why they are observed by the church. Much of the material here will come *from* a book called *The Baptist Faith and Message* by Herschel Hobbs. This would be a good book for you to check out of your church library, or to add to your own library. It is available in Lifeway book stores.

BAPTISM

Christian baptism is the immersing of a believer in water. It is done in the name of the Father, the Son, and the Holy Spirit. The word in Greek, the language of the New Testament, is *baptisma*. The root word, *baptizo* means to "plunge, or submerge or immerse". Therefore Southern Baptists practice immersion, or dipping the person to be baptized under the water.

Probably the most important thing to remember is that baptism doesn't save anyone. It is simply a symbol, portraying the death, burial, and resurrection of Jesus Christ. You don't have to be baptized to be saved. However, you would certainly want to be baptized not only to show others in a public way that you are now a Christian, but also because it is a very meaningful experience for you to remember the rest of your lifetime. It is also necessary for membership in the local church.

Prior to Jesus himself being baptized, John the Baptist was preaching for people to repent, to turn their lives around, to change the way that they lived, to be aware of their sinful nature, and to do something about it. Jesus did not need to repent. He had done nothing wrong, but He did want people to recognize John the Baptist's ministry and to set an example for His followers. John the Baptist's mother was Jesus' mother's cousin. He was sent by God to announce the coming of Jesus. He played an important part in preparing the way for Jesus, including baptizing Jesus in the River Jordan (See Matthew 3:16).

There are a couple of Bible passages that talk about repentance and baptism and being saved. But the preponderance of Scripture talks only of repentance to be saved (Luke 13:2-9; Acts 16:27-34; Romans 10:8-10). *Read these now.* Because of these Scriptures, Southern Baptists feel that repentance and belief in Jesus Christ are what saves us and that baptism, although not necessary for salvation, is our way of saying to others, "I have accepted Christ as my Savior and am going to follow Him."

Some people might refer you to Mark 16:16, but the best old manuscripts end with the eighth verse in this chapter, and we feel that the remaining verses in that chapter were added later.

I cannot understand why anyone would not want to be baptized. Jesus was baptized. He was immersed, and I want to be as much like Him as I possibly can be.

In addition to that, as stated previously, Southern Baptist churches require baptism for membership into the local church. Whether you are a new Christian or a member of another denomination where immersion is not required, membership in the local Southern Baptist Church is granted only after you have been baptized. If you have been baptized by immersion in another denomination, you will find the rule varies from one church to another. Some will require baptism, although you may have been immersed, while others will accept immersion from some other denominations.

We do not believe that pouring or sprinkling is sufficient. Sprinkling became a matter of convenience when some churches decided they would bring infants into the church.

Certainly that would simplify a lot of things, but what good would it do in the long run? Infants cannot make decisions to follow Christ. Infants cannot make decisions to repent, to turn their lives around. The Bible tells us plainly in those verses you just read that belief and repentance are necessary for salvation. The mere fact that infants have been sprinkled does not save them. The same is true of baptism. If a child, teenager, or adult is pressured into baptism without a firm belief and commitment to repent, nothing has been accomplished. Romans 10:9 says, "That if you confess with your mouth, Jesus is Lord, and believe in your heart that God raised Him from the dead, you will be saved."

Most Baptist churches have their own baptismal pool located in the front of the sanctuary. The pastor or a staff member will contact you about a date to be baptized. The pastor may want you to complete this book or some other training materials before he baptizes you, just to be sure you understand the significance of what you are doing. It is a good time to invite friends and relatives to witness the event, and if they are not saved, it should provide an opportunity for you to share with them why you are being baptized.

The pastor will probably meet with you before the baptism to show you how to stand and to describe the procedure so that things go smoothly during the service. That way you will know what to expect.

Remember that baptism will not save you, but it is required for membership in a Southern Baptist Church. Christ wants you to be baptized. In the last words He gave to His disciples before He ascended back into heaven, He said, "Therefore, go and make disciples of all nations, *baptizing them* in the name of the Father and of the Son and of the Holy Spirit, and teaching them to obey everything I have commanded you" (Matthew 28:19-20). It is His command. It is our duty and privilege to obey.

Now let's talk about the Lord's Supper.

THE LORD'S SUPPER

The night before Jesus was crucified, He met with the disciples to observe the Feast of Unleavened Bread. This was the first day of the Passover, the celebration of the time when the Israelites were captive in Egypt. Moses was chosen by God to lead them out of captivity and to the Promised Land. Pharaoh, the Egyptian ruler, was not agreeable to the idea of approximately one million slaves and their children leaving the country. So God sent a series of plagues to persuade Pharaoh to let the Israelites go. He was still not convinced, so as a last resort God struck down the firstborn in each Egyptian family.

Each Israelite family killed a lamb and marked the doorpost of their house with the blood of the lamb so that when the Lord passed through the land, He would see the blood on the doorpost and know in which homes to spare the eldest child. He passed them over, and this is where the term Passover came from. You can read about it in detail in Exodus 3-12.

Every year for centuries, all orthodox Jews have observed the Passover. Jesus and His disciples followed that tradition and met together to observe the Passover supper on the proper Thursday evening. You can read about this in Mark 14:1-25. Take time to read this passage now.

You will note that in the seventeenth verse, Jesus brings up the subject of His betrayal by one of the disciples. He knew that His time had come to be sacrificed on the cross.

As they were eating, Jesus took bread from the table and broke it, said a prayer, and gave a piece to each of the disciples. He showed His willingness to sacrifice His body for our sins as He told them, "Take it. This is my body." He was saying to them, "I willingly give up my body for you."

Then He took the cup, evidently the juice of the grape. The Bible says the fruit of the vine. In Matthew 26: 27-29, it gives us more detail of what Jesus said. They used a communal cup, and as Jesus passed the cup to them, He said, "Drink from it, all of you. This is my blood of the covenant, which is poured out for many for the forgiveness of sins."

He was saying, "I voluntarily give up my blood so that your sins can be forgiven even before they happen." His body and His blood would be sacrificed on the cross so that our sins would be forgiven. He would make the ultimate sacrifice, the sacrifice of a sinless man for the sins of all those who would believe in Him.

Now turn in your Bible to 1 Corinthians 11:23-29. Note that in the twenty-fifth verse Christ is quoted as saying, "Do this in remembrance of me." And so here we have the command for the second ordinance, the Lord's Supper.

Southern Baptists believe that the bread and the fruit of the vine are symbols of Jesus' body and blood. Roman Catholics believe in *transubstantiation*, or in other words, that the bread and the fruit of the vine miraculously become Christ's body and blood. Others believe in con-substantiation, which is a modified view.

I think Dr. Hobbs in *The Baptist Faith and Message* explains it quite well. "When Jesus said, 'This is my body' and 'This is my blood' (Matt. 26:26, 28), He no more meant that they actually became such than by saying 'I am the door' (John 10:9) or that He was a hole in a wall or a piece of wood. In all cases He spoke symbolically. So the elements are merely symbols of His body and blood."[1]

You may be in a church where the Lord's Supper is observed every month, or you may be in a church where it is only once a quarter. This will vary from one church to another. The important thing to remember is that this is a time for you to reflect seriously on your life and how well you are serving your Lord. It is also a time to call to remembrance the tremendous sacrifice that Christ made for each of us when He willingly went to the cross, enduring pain, agony, and humiliation for the salvation of us all.

The deacons usually assist the pastor in serving the Lord's Supper, and you will normally remain in your seat as the elements (bread and fruit of the vine) are passed to you.

If you are visiting in another church and they observe the Lord's Supper while you are there, you should ask someone if it is all right for you to participate. Some churches observe what is termed "closed communion," which means it is only for the members of their church. Most churches, however, will welcome you to participate.

I hope this has provided you with the information you need to know about the two ordinances of the church and that you will always appreciate the significance of them as you worship.

Endnotes

1 Hobbs, *Baptist Faith and Message* (Convention Press, 1971), p.76.

CHAPTER 10

Southern Baptists—
Who Are They?

By this point in your reading, it has probably become obvious to you that there are some considerable differences from one denomination to another. The question probably has entered your mind as to how can churches be so different when they all started with the same Bible? Why isn't there just one denomination where God's Word is studied and observed.

I, for one, wish that it were so. What a tremendous impact we could make on the world for Christ if we all were working together to spread His Word—if all the funds contributed could go toward one administration, one corps of missionaries, one group of seminaries!

But people are different. They interpret things differently. They like to worship in different ways. Some people like a warm, friendly atmosphere in worship, while others choose a more formal, structured worship service. The reasons for difference are almost endless, and we don't have time to discuss them all here. What I want to do in this chapter is to give you a little of the background of Southern Baptists. Then, in the next chapter, we will talk about the organization of the local church, the state convention, and the national organization that now spans the globe in its outreach. Let's start with a little history.

I have had some people question why I wanted to put history into this book. Some younger people in particular raised the question, "Why, when many churches are trying to identify less with any certain denomination, do you want to put in a chapter on history?"

Let me answer real briefly. The Bible itself is a book of history. Even though the last of the Bible was written over 1900 years ago, the history of the church continues.

We owe an eternal debt of gratitude to the many who oftentimes sacrificed their lives and their families in service to God. And how can we not be interested in how God has continued to work down through the years to insure that His Word is preached and lost people are saved?

I, for one, am grateful for our history. I hope that you are too. It isn't always pleasant. There are incidents that have occurred "in the name of Christianity" that are certainly not pleasing to God. Things have happened that sometimes assault our senses, but it is history, and we owe it to ourselves to know a little of that history. So let me move on.

"In the beginning was the Word, and the Word was with God, and the Word was God" John (1:1).

Where does the history of anything start? It has to start with God. "All things were made by Him and without Him was not anything made that was made" (John 1:3).

God has a plan. He has had a plan from the beginning of time. This has been true for Southern Baptists down through the years. I can't begin to tell the story of Southern Baptists in a few paragraphs. I would refer you to the following books if you are a history buff and would like to know about the heritage of Southern Baptists: *The Indomitable Baptists,* by O.K.

and Marjorie Moore Armstrong; *A Short History of the Baptists,* by Henry C. Vedder; *The Southern Baptist Convention and Its People,* by Robert Baker; *and Flowers and Fruits From the Wilderness,* by Z.N. Morrell. I also included most of this material in a history of the First Baptist Church in Marble Falls, Texas, *Thee First One Hundred Years.*

The Old Testament tells the story of man's failure to atone for his wrongdoings down through the ages. Sacrifices placed on the altar were often the poorest of the flock or the crops rather than the best, as God required. For long periods of time, God's people completely forgot about Him. Then there would be a great awakening, a rededication, and then again a falling away. Read 2 Chronicles from the tenth chapter to the end, and you will get the picture real quickly.

Two thousand years ago, God, knowing man, by his own feeble efforts, would never bridge the gap between himself and God, sent His Son as the ultimate sacrifice. Jesus became our mediator, our Savior.

The Bible tells us that Jesus was immersed in the River Jordan. A few years later, Philip, obeying God's command, immersed the Ethiopian whom he had witnessed to. Baptism by immersion was commonplace in the early church.

The church of the apostles was very Baptistic. Those who believed in Christ as their Savior and were immersed became members of the early church. But the majority of the Jewish people never accepted Christ as their Messiah. Read Acts 28:17 to the end of the chapter. You will see that Paul recognized this, and in obedience, he started being a missionary to the rest of the world. And from this beginning God reached out to you and to me.

But by the middle of the third century, the church was headquartered in Rome, and many changes were taking place. Baptism became a requirement for salvation, and for the sake of convenience, immersion was replaced with sprinkling. Babies were baptized at an early age before they had any knowledge of God or salvation. Although God's Word states specifically that we are to "confess with our mouth," this requirement was ignored.

There are some who would dispute the written history and claim that for the next twelve hundred years there was a direct descendancy of those who believed in immersion and a profession of faith, but there is almost no written history to support this claim.

We do know that in A.D. 1170 in France, Peter Waldo founded a sect of believers who practiced the tradition of the early Christians:

a) baptism of believers

b) autonomy of the local church

c) democratic congregational procedures.

The Waldensians, as they were called, became an object of persecution, and most of them moved to the Alps, where we find the first churches recorded since the time of the apostles, that followed what we would call Baptist beliefs.

Other nonconformist groups were to follow, and in most cases they suffered persecution and death because of their beliefs. They felt they should be allowed to interpret the Scripture for themselves and to worship as they pleased.[1]

In 1320, John Wycliffe was born in England. He believed that people should be able to read the Scripture for themselves, that Christ was the head of the church, and that there was no need for a mediator. [2]

John Huss, another dissenter, a Bohemian priest, was burned at the stake for asserting that the Scripture should be the Christian's supreme guide.[3]

And in 1517, Martin Luther, a German priest, nailed a protest to the door of the chapel, and the reforming of the Christian church became headline news.[4]

John Calvin, born in 1509 in France, and who spent most of his life in Switzerland, became a great theologian. He said it was man's right to have direct communication with God.[5]

You don't have to be a history buff to get excited over God's fulfillment of His plan from that point forward. In 1525, a man named Conrad Grebel, who lived in Zurich, was studying under a rebellious Catholic priest named Ulrich Zwingli. Zwingli had become well-versed in God's Scripture and had come to the conclusion that infant baptism was not scriptural.

As Grebel and others studied under Zwingli, they became known as Humanists. The group decided that they wanted to be rebaptized. Zwingli refused to go along with their request, so they broke ranks with him and started their own group. They poured water over each other's heads as a means of rebaptizing themselves. They were known as the Swiss Brethren.[6]

The Swiss Brethren grew and soon a derisive term was coined for them. They were called Anabaptists, or baptizers again.

Anabaptists wanted to be free to worship with no interference from the state. They wanted to baptize believers who understood the true significance of the ordinance. They felt it was the believer's responsibility to make up the church and govern it and to spread the Gospel. The Scriptures supported their beliefs.

In 1530, a Dutch priest named Menno Simons found himself struggling with his faith. He studied the works of the Anabaptists. In 1531, his brother and 300 other Anabaptists were killed in cold blood, massacred by order of the emperor in the Netherlands.

Menno Simons could no longer tolerate living with what he considered to be an incomplete or false faith. So he too became an Anabaptist. He escaped arrest by traveling across Holland and Germany, preaching and writing tracts. His followers became known as Mennonites. Many of them migrated to England, only to find opposition there from the Church of England.[7]

In the 1530s, Henry VIII removed the jurisdiction of the Roman Catholic Church from power in England and established the Church of England. He began to persecute the Mennonites and Anabaptists. He had fourteen Anabaptists burned at the stake. Many others were arrested. At the same time, he had dissent within his own ranks. A group within the Church of England demanded that the Church of England be "purified." They demanded a simpler worship service and strict austerity in personal lives. They insisted that the Scripture be the authority for doctrine and rites. They became known as Puritans.[8]

An Anglican minister, Robert Browne, demanded that the local congregations be free from each other, each as a democracy unto itself.

In 1594, John Smyth was ordained in the Church of England. He became a Puritan, and because of his differences with the Church, he left the church and became a medical doctor in Gainsborough. The local priest was very inactive, so Dr. Smyth founded his own congregation.

In the early 1600s, the new ruler in England, King James, sponsored the production of the King James version of the Bible. He also intensified the persecution of the Anabaptists and other Separatist groups, causing Smyth and his followers to flee to Amsterdam. There, Smyth created a new congregation based on Scripture. They were given the name "The Church of the Baptists." This is the first known record of a church group known as Baptists. This happened in 1609. In 1611, Thomas Helwys took ten of the members and moved back to England. They established a church near London called "Ye Baptiste Church."[9]

Roger Williams was born in 1603 in England. His family lived near the Newgate prison, which was a favored site for the execution of heretics. Through the experience of seeing some of these executions, Roger developed a deep sense of pity for the Christians who were martyred there. Williams later studied for the ministry. While he was attending Cambridge, and through the influence of Sir Edward Coke, Roger became interested in the Puritans. When Sir Edward was incarcerated and another Puritan publicly whipped and a brand put on his face, Roger had had enough. He identified himself as a Baptist, wrote a letter of dissent to the Archbishop, and before he could be arrested, he and his bride sailed for America. That was in 1630.

In America, he was asked to pastor a Puritan church, but he found that the government of Massachusetts believed in a state-supported church. A government-supported church was the reason he had left England. He was quite outspoken in his opposition to this, and after a great deal of trouble in the Massachusetts Commonwealth, Roger and some friends started a village across the river and named it Providence. There, in 1639, Roger Williams founded the Providence Baptist Church, the first Baptist church in America. It is still in existence today.[10] My wife and I worshiped there a few years ago.

Although people had moved to America for religious freedom, many of them wanted freedom only for their own church. Religious intolerance and persecution forced Baptists to move into new areas. Some, who had been persecuted in Maine, moved to South Carolina. By 1700, there were fourteen Baptist churches in the colonies, and by 1701 there were five Baptist churches in Philadelphia alone. These Philadelphia churches formed the first association of churches but carefully maintained their individual autonomy. By 1800, South Carolina had the first association formed in the South, and Virginia had over 400 Baptist churches.[11]

In 1780, Robert Raikes started teaching the Bible in his home to boys from the slums in Gloucester, England. Five years later, William Fox started a Sunday school in England, but many preachers opposed Sunday school as not being scriptural. It was 1815 before three ladies started the first

Sunday school in the U.S. at the First Baptist Church in Philadelphia, Pennsylvania.[12]

By 1793, William Carey had become the first foreign missionary for the Baptist faith, and by 1814, Baptists had developed a foreign mission body.

In 1845 a sharp division began to develop among U.S. Baptists. Representation on the mission boards and the slavery issue were the main causes of dissent. The end result was a split between Southern and Northern Baptists. For many years you would find Southern Baptist churches only in the southern United States. Over a period of time, Southern Baptist churches started opening in the North, and Northern Baptists changed the name of their convention to The American Baptist Convention. Today there are a few scattered American Baptist churches in the South, but Southern Baptists now have churches all across the United States and in Canada. Southern Baptist missionaries have established churches all across the world. Vermont was the last state to have a Southern Baptist church located there, and that church was established in 1963. Serious efforts have been made in the past several years to enlist black churches to join with Southern Baptists, and this has met with good success.

In 1996, 379,344 people were baptized in Southern Baptist churches in the United States, and 283,674 were baptized in Southern-Baptist related churches overseas. This means that one baptism occurred every forty-eight seconds. On the average, four new Southern Baptist churches are started every day. Of course, there are also some churches that close each year due to population shifts from rural to urban, but in 1997 there were 40,613 Southern Baptist churches.[13]

That is a brief history of how Southern Baptists came into being. There is more to the story, and I would encourage you to read some of the history books mentioned at the first of this chapter. As I stated before, you need to read The Baptist

Faith and Message for a clear understanding of what Southern Baptists believe.

In the meantime, I want us to look at Southern Baptists, how they are organized, and what their role is in today's world. We'll do that in the next chapter.

Endnotes

1 Armstrong, *The Indomitable Baptists* (Doubleday, 1967), pp.19-20.

2 Ibid, p.19.

3 Ibid.

4 Ibid.

5 Ibid.

6 Ibid, pp. 20-21.

7 Ibid, pp. 28-29.

8 Ibid.

9 Ibid, p .33.

10 Ibid, pp. 50-51.

11 Baker, *The Southern Baptist Convention and Its People,* (Broadman 1975), p.162.

12 Armstrong, op.cit. p. 162.

13 Meet Southern Baptists brochure (Exec. Comm. S.Bap. Conv, 1997), pp. 3-4.

CHAPTER 11

How Southern Baptists Are Organized

Southern Baptist organization almost defies description. A person holding a Masters Degree in Business Administration would shake his head in disbelief. He would say, "There is no way that will work," but it does. As you can see from the statistics at the end of the last chapter, it works very well, and it is almost constantly changing as new ideas emerge and new goals are set.

We have to go back to our earlier statement about each church being autonomous. In theory, we are a theocracy. You will hear people say we are a true democracy. That is not true. We are not a democracy, in which the people rule, but a theocracy, in which Christ is the head of the church.

Everything should be done under God's direction. Each church operates independently and is supposed to seek God's will in making decisions. It is true that the churches are autonomous or self-governed. It is also true that in a well-organized Baptist church, the members vote on any decisions to be made. However, in some churches there may be an individual or some strong-willed group who make many of the decisions. This is not God's intent.

A local church is a group of professing believers in Christ who have been baptized and who have organized themselves for the purpose of doing God's will. Read 1 Peter 2:4-8. Christ is the "capstone" or cornerstone. He is the foundation of the church and its head. Read Ephesians 5:23-24. Note that Christ is the head of the church, and the church is to submit to Christ. Look at one more passage, Colossians 1:10-20; that sums it up very well. Christ is the head of the body, the church. All things were created by Him and for Him, and He is before all things. That is how the church is to operate, with Christ as its head. All other roles in the church are to be subservient to Him. Nothing should be done that is not in His will and that does not glorify Him.

Many churches start out as missions from a larger church in their vicinity. There may be several years of financial and spiritual guidance provided by a larger church before the new church is duly constituted.

You will find that Southern Baptist churches are not all alike. If you were to discuss all Southern Baptist churches, it would take several volumes to discuss the organizational structure and how decisions are made. We don't have time for that, and I'm sure you would quit reading long before we finished, so for our purpose we will discuss the ideal situation and hope that the church you belong to falls into that category.

Christ is the head of the church (Colossians 1:18). We have already looked at that. Christ is the head: the church is the body. They all function as one unit, but the head makes the decisions. In the course *Experiencing God*, Henry Blackaby says we need to see where God is working and join Him in that work.[1] A church that is functioning as it should does not just decide to do something and plunge in. It looks to see where God is at work, then it prays for His leadership and joins Him in the work He is doing. Christ is the Head of the Church.

The pastor is the under-shepherd. In a properly functioning church, he is the local leader. He has the training and experience to provide leadership in following what God would have that local body of believers to do. First Timothy 3:1-6 describes his duties as the overseer. First Timothy 5:17-20 and Titus 1:5-2:8 tell the pastor (elder) (minister) his responsibilities. You will also find in these passages the qualifications that a pastor ought to have.

In a Southern Baptist church, the pastor is employed by the church. A pulpit or search committee is elected by the church, and it seeks out the names of persons the committee feel are qualified. If the committee feels a person is qualified, they will interview him. After the interview, they may invite him to come and preach on a given Sunday. The congregation votes on whether or not they want to employ that person as their pastor, hopefully after a great deal of prayer.

In a small congregation, the pastor may be the only person on the staff. In most cases he is paid by the congregation, but he may pastor without pay, or in the case of a small mission church, another church may be covering the expenses. In some small churches, the pastor may be what is called a bivocational pastor. This means that he works in a secular job at least part of the week to help support his family. In some very small congregations, there simply isn't enough money to pay the rent on the building and a salary to the pastor. Sometimes in those situations the pastor draws no salary.

As congregations grow in size, there is a wide variance in staff personnel. Usually the second person added is a secretary. Then comes a minister of music and education. This person leads the congregational singing and may organize a small choir. He will also recruit the teachers for Sunday school and see that the literature for Bible study is ordered. As the church continues to grow, the minister of music will become a full-time job. A large choir, children's choirs, a handbell choir, and perhaps an orchestra all become a part of the music minister's duties. In many larger churches, a large-scale music presentation is produced at Easter or Christmas under his direction. In many churches the minister of music will also plan the worship service, choosing hymns, choruses, and the order of the service.

At the point that the music becomes a fulltime job, a minister of education will likely be added. The person who is hired for this position will have responsibility for all types of training, including the Sunday school and discipleship training, which can include a variety of methods of educating members of the church. The minister of education may also be responsible for some of the church's visitation to prospects, shut-ins, and those in the hospital. Of course, the pastor will usually lead in those efforts.

As the church continues to grow, a minister to youth, a minister for outreach, children's department directors, and others may be added to the pastoral staff. These additions call for more secretaries, maintenance personnel, and musicians. Eventually, the church payroll may include a fairly large number of people.

In almost every Baptist church, you will find a board of deacons. This is a group of laypeople who are elected by the church to serve. The word *deacon* is derived from the word *diakonos*, which is a Greek word that means servant. Deacons fulfill that role somewhat differently in different churches. One of their primary roles should be to serve the congregation through visitation of the members, praying for them, and providing encouragement. They will also assist the pastor in serving the Lord's Supper.

In some congregations, each deacon is assigned a certain number of families to minister to. Deacons may pay particular attention to the elderly. The deacons in most churches meet once a month. They will usually discuss matters pertaining to the church. If these items require formal action, they will then be recommended to the entire church for a vote. This could involve anything from building new buildings to hiring a new custodian.

In most churches, the recommendations for almost all items to be voted on start in a committee. A committee on committees is elected, and it in turn asks people to serve on various standing committees in the church. One group may have the responsibility for producing a budget for the new year. Another may handle personnel matters, the hiring of secretaries, custodial workers, pianists, and so on. Another committee may be responsible for the buildings that house the church. When a committee has a recommendation regarding its sphere of responsibility, it will normally bring this to the deacons, who will then take it to the entire church for a vote.

If an isolated situation occurs, an ad hoc committee may be named to take care of that special item, and here again it will recommend a solution for the church to vote on.

Many churches also elect a board of trustees who are responsible for handling the finances of the church, but still not without the vote of the church.

Most Baptist churches hold a monthly business meeting. The day and time will vary, but the most usual time is Wednesday or Sunday evening. All church members are eligible to vote, and this is where final decisions are made. These sessions should be prayerful, seeking God's will. They should be harmonious. They should not be contests of wills, but times when the church honestly seeks out God's will for the matter at hand. If His will cannot be very plainly determined, then the matter should be postponed until His will becomes obvious.

That is a fairly simple explanation of how the local church operates. As I mentioned earlier, this will vary from one church to another, but the basics should be there.

Of course, there are many areas of the local church's work that can best be provided by a larger organization. Preparing

Bible study materials, sending out missionaries, starting churches in new areas, and many other support items can best be done by people trained in those particular specialties. That is why Southern Baptists have developed support organizations to provide these services.

There are three support groups that we need to talk about, the association, the state convention, and the national convention.

THE ASSOCIATION

The association is comprised of churches in a fairly close geographical area. In the U.S., it may be the churches in one county or many counties, depending on the population density. In Canada, the association includes an entire province. The association has no governing capacity over the local church. Its function is strictly one of support. The association is led by the association missionary. In most cases, he will have had experience for several years as a pastor before he is called to this duty. He may have one secretary or several assistants, depending on the size of the association. It is impossible to discuss all that the association might do, but among its principal duties are helping a church without a pastor to find some interim help and referring names of pastors seeking a church. It is also available to give advice on new buildings, acquisition of land, programs in the church that may need strengthening, or new programs the church may be considering.

Many associations will have associates who are knowledgeable in Christian education, or they may have persons skilled in starting new churches. In bilingual areas or multi-ethnic areas, there may be a specialist who can assist minority groups in forming new churches and finding other well-established churches who would support a new work financially. In most associations, the pastors and staff in the local churches meet together monthly for fellowship, exchange of information, and encouragement.

Many associations will also coordinate the work of volunteer missionaries who may be involved in prison ministries, elderly ministries, or other similar tasks. The Mission Service Corps is a large group of volunteers from churches all over the country who commit two years, oftentimes in their retirement years, to ministries supervised by associations.

Once a year, representatives of each church in the association meet together and provide the association with a report on the activities of their church for the past year. This report is called the church letter. At this meeting a vote will be held on any business that needs to be taken care of by the association as well as pass a budget for the next year. We will talk about how the association is funded in chapter 12.

STATE CONVENTION

The statewide support group is usually called a convention. It may be the Baptist General Convention of (state), or a similar name. Here again, the leader is normally a pastor with many years of experience, and in most states he will have a rather large staff. There will be a statewide coordinator of all the women's and men's groups in the local churches. There will usually be a director of evangelism or outreach. Most state conventions will sponsor some form of higher education, one or more church-related colleges and/or universities. Their work will also include a ministry to orphaned, needy, or abused children. In some states you will also find Baptist-sponsored health and retirement facilities.

The state conventions exist to encourage and assist churches, associations and institutions, and other Baptist entities in fulfilling the Great Commission of the Lord Jesus Christ.

Most state conventions also sponsor "Partnership Missions" with a foreign country over a period of one or more years to assist the missionaries in those countries with volunteer personnel and other needs. We will talk a little more about this in the last chapter.

State conventions provide expertise in music, education,

children's work, and other areas of ministry. And we probably haven't begun to cover all the work of the state convention.

Shortly after the associations meet each year to give their annual report, the state convention meets to conduct business, adopt a budget, accept reports from the associations, and provide motivation for those in attendance. Each church is entitled to representation at this meeting. Again, we will discuss how the state convention is funded in the next chapter.

Most states have a state newspaper that carries news of Baptists in the state, and some national and international news of Baptist interest. In some cases the newspaper is customized for individual churches with a page of local church news.

THE SOUTHERN BAPTIST CONVENTION

Finally, we come to the Southern Baptist Convention. Since its beginning in 1845, the Southern Baptist Convention has become the largest denomination of believers in the United States except for the Roman Catholic Church.

Here again it is a support organization—this time on an international scale. Don't feel that because it concerns God's church that it is archaic or old fashioned. In 1997 the entire structure of the Southern Baptist Convention was reviewed and restructured to make it more cost-effective, and we hope to help it reach more people for Christ in the years to come.

The Southern Baptist Convention is divided into twelve divisions. I don't want to get into too much detail here. I would like to give you a glimpse into some of the things that Southern Baptists are doing to support their churches and to reach out across the world to those who have not yet had an opportunity to accept Jesus Christ as their Savior. Let's look at some of these organizations.

Heading up this work is the *Executive Committee.* This committee is made up of eighty-one members who are elected at the national convention, which meets in a different city every fall. The President/Chief Executive Officer of the Executive Committee is nominated by a search committee and then affirmed by the convention. This committee oversees all the work that goes on in the convention and also has the responsibility for promoting the Cooperative Program, which will be discussed in chapter 12.

Lifeway Christian Resources of the Southern Baptist Convention is the training arm for laypeople in our convention. It produces Sunday school, Bible study, discipleship training, and other literature. Baptist Heritage, stewardship education, church-growth work, and ministry to men and women are some of the many areas the board is responsible for. They also provide help in church architecture and training for church secretaries. It also operates two conference centers at Glorieta, New Mexico, and Ridgecrest, North Carolina. Its office is in Nashville, Tennessee.

The responsibility for mission work is divided into two categories. **The North American Mission Board** has almost five thousand missionaries across the United States, Canada, American Samoa, Puerto Rico, and the Virgin Islands. Its responsibilities include church planting, evangelism, literacy training, hunger relief, and prayer for spiritual awakening. This group also includes the work of the Brotherhood Commission (men's work in the local churches and their outreach), and the Radio and Television Commission. The headquarters for the North American Mission Board is Atlanta, Georgia.

The North American mission Board Publishes on Mission Magazine.

The International Mission Board supports over four thousand two hundred missionaries in one hundred twenty-six nations. Its work is similar in nature to that of the North American Mission Board, with a strong emphasis on church planting. Its interest is all of the world outside North America.

Theological seminaries have been set up in many foreign countries to train local pastors. This frees the missionaries to go and start more new churches. I had the pleasure of working for three weeks with a couple who were church planters in Tanzania. They had started thirty-six churches back in the bush, and when I was there, they had pastors for almost all of those churches.

The International Mission Board publishes a magazine called Commission, which is very informative, telling about what is happening on the mission fields around the world.

The work of the board is divided into fourteen geographical areas of the world. Its main office is in Richmond, Virginia.

The **Southern Baptist Seminaries** division is responsible for the six seminaries located across the southern United States and California. These seminaries are the training facilities for pastors, ministers of education, ministers of music, youth ministers, missionaries, and those who want to broaden their knowledge of the Bible and become more adept at leadership in their churches. Masters degrees and doctorates are the advanced degrees generally granted. In addition, lay members of the church who have a special interest can take one or more courses at the various seminary extension centers located in several other cities.

Early in Southern Baptist history, a group of women started a campaign to raise money for foreign missions. The effort was named after a lady missionary to China, Lottie Moon. That organization today is known as the **Women's Missionary Union,** and in many local churches you will find a group of dedicated women whose primary interest is raising funds for our missionaries and educating the members of their churches about mission work. If it were not for their work down through the years, mission work in the Southern Baptist Convention would not be nearly as advanced. Their headquarters is in Birmingham, Alabama.

The **Annuity Board** handles the investment of retirement funds for pastors and staff personnel. Most churches provide an amount to be invested as one of the pastor and staff's fringe benefits. The Annuity Board is located in Dallas, Texas.

The Ethics and Religious Liberty Commission makes contacts with legislative forces in our government and other governments to try to protect religious freedom and to encourage legislative bodies to follow God's will. It is headquartered in Nashville, Tennessee.

A driving force behind all of this is the commitment of Southern Baptists to a program called BOLD MISSION THRUST. This is a program dedicated to reach the entire world with the Gospel by the year 2000. To help accomplish this, goals have been set for the number of baptisms, churches to be started, Sunday school or Bible study enrollment, missionary appointments, and number of short-term volunteer missionaries assigned.[2]

This should give you an idea of the involvement of Southern Baptists in trying to reach the world for Christ. It should also show you that your tithe or offering is not being squandered, but is quickly and efficiently put to good use. In the next chapter we will talk about where the money comes from to support the vast amount of work carried out by Southern Baptists.

Endnotes

1 Blackaby & King, *Experiencing God;* (Lifeway, 1990), p.15.
2 *Meet Southern Baptists,* op. cit., pp. 2-4.

CHAPTER 12

Where the Money Comes From

*I*t is obvious from the last chapter that an organization covering so many areas on local, state, national, and foreign levels requires a large amount of capital. Pastors, staff members, rent, utilities, missionaries, and the myriad of support personnel all have to be paid. So where does the money come from?

It comes from God. That may sound mystical or supernatural, but it is not. God is the source of all our needs. He provides both physical and spiritual sustenance. First Corinthians 2:14 says, "The natural man receiveth not the things of the Spirit of God for they are foolishness unto Him. Nor can he know these things because they must be spiritually discerned." But as we take part with God in His work, we receive the things of the Spirit, which help us to be more effective.

It is important for Christians to remember that God owns it all. He created everything. It belongs to Him, and He provides it for our use. This is a completely different concept than that held by the average person on the street. According to them, they earned every penny they have without help from anyone, and they are going to do with it whatever they want to, whatever way gives them the most gratification.

Christian people feel otherwise. They know that it all belongs to God. John 1:3 says, "Through Him all things were made; without Him nothing was made that has been made." God's ownership of everything includes me, and it includes you. Second Corinthians 1:21-22 says, "Now it is God who makes both us and you stand firm in Christ. He anointed us, set His seal of ownership on us and put His Spirit in our hearts as a deposit, guaranteeing what is to come." He created us. He has a plan for our lives. If we are willing to yield ourselves to Him, He can do great things through us. But first of all we must acknowledge that it all belongs to Him, including ourselves.

We talked earlier about Christians hurting. We need to understand that Christians do hurt sometimes, physically or financially. Many times we bring this pain on ourselves by spending too much, charging too much on credit cards or other types of credit, which includes buying things we don't need. I don't want you to get the impression that God will give us everything we want or ask for. He will take care of us, but what He sees as our needs and our idea of what we want are two different things.

Remember this, though: if He is willing to create us and claim us as His children (Read Romans 8:12-17), then we should be willing to give back to Him a small part of what He has given to us. Did you read those verses in Romans? Do you understand what it says? When we become Christians, we become the children of God, heirs, along with Jesus Christ to all that He has. This will be what we will share in eternity. He has given all of that to us, and He expects us to help promote His work here, help the needy and the lost (those without Christ), and see to it that His church thrives in this world.

Understand that He doesn't need our help. He owns it all, and He can sustain it without our meager part. But He is testing us to see if we are good stewards. The Bible is full of stories that indicate this. In the very first book, (Genesis 4:3-7), Cain and Abel are tested to see if they will give a pleasing sacrifice. Jesus tells several parables about the use and investment of what the Father has given us (Luke 12:16-21). Paul exhorts the churches to be generous in their gifts to help the church in Jerusalem, which was in need. Second Corinthians 8-9 are two chapters you need to read now.

You will hear the word "fellowship" used a lot around Baptist churches. The word means "to take part with." The Bible says we are to join in fellowship with God, or in other words to take part with Him. He shares with us and we share with Him.

Many people outside the church look on the church as a group of people always asking for money. They joke about it without realizing all of the good being done in the community and around the world by the church. As you saw in chapter 11, much more is involved than just paying a pastor a salary. If all of the churches quit doing charity work, the effect on the needy would be disastrous. Those who think all of the money contributed into the church is spent locally are completely misinformed.

You may find examples of people in the church who collect large sums of money and then use it for themselves, particularly in some TV ministries, but I believe these are isolated cases. As we look at how Southern Baptists give their money and then distribute it, you will see that integrity is a priority.

The support of God's work all starts with you and God. God blesses you with His provision and allows you to share in His ministry. Nowhere in the New Testament are you told how much you are to give. In the Old Testament, the tithe (10%) was expected. In fact, the tithe probably was much more, because the 10% referred to several different offerings.

It probably amounted to 23% of their income. You will find that most churches today still talk about the tithe, and it is encouraged in some of the training materials you will see. I believe most Christian leaders today would agree that 10% should be the minimum, and you will find people who give a great deal more.

You may already be committed to house and car payments that would keep you from giving 10%. If that is true, figure out a percentage of your gross income that you can give, whether it is 2% or 8%, and then do some budgeting so that as you pay off some of your debts you can increase your giving a percentage point or so a year.

You may be saying, "I have a waiting list of things that I need to buy. If I give ten percent to church I'll never have the things I want." Let me answer this way. If we allow God to define our needs, He may feel differently about that new car than we do. He may show us that those new clothes can wait, or that we don't need quite as large a home as we would like to have. Try tithing. You will find that pleasing God will give you a lot more satisfaction than worrying about yourself and all of your wants.

We are supposed to glorify God in all that we do, but many Christian people fall down in the area of stewardship in several ways. They take on too much debt, they use their credit cards indiscriminately, or they just want too many things. As a result, they fail to do what God wants them to do, and this does not glorify Him.

God is also not glorified when we argue in front of the children over finances, or when we file bankruptcy because our greed glands were working overtime. I believe Romans 12:1-2 should be the motto of all Christians when dealing with their finances. "Therefore, I urge you brothers, in view of God's mercy, to offer your bodies as living sacrifices, holy and pleasing to God—this is your spiritual act of worship. Do not conform any longer to the pattern of this world, but be transformed by the renewing of your mind. Then you will be able to test and approve what God's will is—-His good, pleasing and perfect will."

We cannot go on spending like there is no tomorrow, give a pittance or nothing at all to God, and still glorify Him. Our lives need to be changed. Debt should be virtually eliminated as soon as possible. The only possible exception might be the mortgage on our home. This may take a while, but it will free us up to serve God in a way we never dreamed possible. The interest we save by not having time payments amounts to a large sum of money, and in many cases, the interest saved will pay our tithe. If we need help in the area of managing our finances, we can almost always find someone in our church with expertise who can give us sound financial wisdom. The word "budget" is not a dirty word. We plan all other areas of our life. Why not do some thinking and planning on how best to use our resources? Don't be afraid or ashamed to ask for help if you have never budgeted before. It proves to those around us that we are serious about serving God.

So we start by giving our money to our local church. Whether it is a small amount or large is not as important as the fact that we are being honest with God. Most churches provide their members with envelopes to put their offering in. There will be a number on each box that identifies the giver and helps the church financial secretary keep track of what we give. At the end of the year, the church will provide everyone a statement of how much they have given during the year so we will have a record for our income taxes. If you have not received a box of envelopes from your church, call the church office and ask for envelopes to be mailed you. Then as we all give, let's see what happens next.

In almost every church, there will be a budget committee. Each year that committee prepares a proposed budget for the following year that will be presented to the church member-ship in a regular or special business meeting. The committee will look at all of the various expenses of the church: salaries, utilities, rent or mortgage payments, building maintenance, advertising (some churches use billboards, newspaper ads, radio broadcasts, or special materials), and the list goes on.

The larger the church, the larger the number of items that may be included—perhaps a day care center or library. The church may provide subscriptions to the state Baptist newspaper for the members. Some churches will have a special page in that paper for local church information.

Salary increases, note payments, and unusual maintenance costs all have to be considered, and many times other committees will need to be consulted. For example, the building maintenance committee should have some input each year on what maintenance work needs to be done in the following year. The personnel committee may have recommendations for raises to be given to various staff members. The missions committee may be planning to start a new mission in the next year, and funds will be needed for that purpose.

All of these items are enumerated in the church budget. The budget committee is one of the busiest committees in the church if it does its job correctly. Personnel costs, insurance for personnel, retirement plans, local mission projects, Bible study, and training materials are all included. Music needs to be purchased for the choir. Church banquets and other functions have to be planned for. Youth camps need to be paid for, and recreation materials purchased. If the church has a bus program to pick up those who can't drive, those costs must be included in the budget.

If you want to see how this works in your church, your church office should have a copy of the budget you can look at. I would suggest you get a copy and study it. It will make you more appreciative of why your church needs everyone to support it financially.

In most church budgets you will also find an item for the support of the association. This may be expressed in a certain amount of dollars, or it may be a percentage of all contributions given to the church through the year. It will be included in the total the church needs to have contributed during the next year.

Then in most churches, either a percentage of the total gifts or a fixed amount is allocated to what Southern Baptists call *The Cooperative Program.* To understand this better, we need to look at the practice of some other denominations.

It has been a custom in some denominations for the local church to send out its own missionaries. If some of its young people feel called to become missionaries, they first obtain their seminary training. Then they are assigned to a mission post by their denomination, or, in some situations, they may choose for themselves where they will serve. The church sends them support checks, or they get individual commitments for support from friends or churches so that they can serve on the mission field, whether in North America or overseas.

Dependence on one local church lead to several problems, too numerous to discuss here. Suffice it to say, it is a method that can provide inadequate support for many missionaries and more-than-sufficient support for a very few. Financial problems in the local church or with the individuals helping them also means problems for the missionaries they support.

There has also been a tradition that in some denominations the Archdiocese or a central office receives funds contributed to the church. It pays the bills and determines how the money contributed will be spent. They also determine who is to pastor each church, and therefore exert a lot of control by being in charge of the money and the pastor.

Southern Baptists have designed what we feel is a more efficient way. Because our churches are autonomous, each church determines how much it will give to support mission causes, its association, and the state and national conventions. Many times this will be a percentage of the total given by the members of the church.

You will find in almost all Southern Baptist Church budgets an item for the Cooperative Program. This item can be a stated amount in dollars or a percentage of the gifts to the church. Each church determines how much this will be. Through the year, as this money is given to the church, a check is forwarded to the state convention. The state convention has beforehand determined its budget and an estimate of what will be received. It takes a percentage of the amount contributed by the churches to meet its budget. The balance is sent to the national convention, where it is again divided between all of the agencies in a manner agreed to before the year begins. In this way, each department of the state and national conventions knows approximately how much it will receive each year. It has its own budgets to determine how much can be allocated for salaries, programs, etc.

That is a simplified description of how the Cooperative Program works. But as you saw in chapter 11, when we talked about the organization of the convention, there are many areas of work for the money to go to, and the Cooperative Program guarantees that each of these divisions is adequately taken care of.

Almost every church has its own peculiarities when you look at its finances. Growing churches in metropolitan areas are always in need of more space. A church can only seat so many people in a sanctuary or a Sunday school classroom. Large, growing churches start a second service and two or more Sunday schools. Some may even have a worship service on Saturday evening. Some churches stretch the facilities as far as they can, and then they have to initiate a building program to accommodate the growth. Some growing churches may have an almost perpetual building fund for expansion so that they can pay as they go. Other churches may sell bonds for a new building and then pay them off with a campaign that can last several years.

We mentioned in chapter 11 about the Lottie Moon Mission Offering. Lottie Moon was born in 1840. In 1873 she went to China and spent thirty-nine years as a missionary in that country. A woman ahead of her time.

Annie Armstrong, who spent most of her life in Baltimore, founded the Women's Missionary Union in 1888. This is commonly known as the W.M.U. She was named the first Corresponding Secretary (president). In addition she ministered to seamen, Africans and Native Americans.

She suggested that the Christmas offering for foreign missions be named for Lottie Moon. In 1895 an Easter offering was inaugurated to supplement Home missions. In 1934 this offering was named for Annie Armstrong because of her long and faithful service to God through the W.M.U.

Most states also have an offering for state missions. In some churches the three special mission offerings are combined into one appeal.

Understand that we will never be coerced into giving. Open your Bible to 2 Corinthians 9:6-15. Read this very carefully. There are three or four sermons there for each of us. Whenever we feel ourselves regretting having to write a check to the church, we need to read these verses again. "God loves a cheerful giver."

It's Up to You

*T*his is the last chapter, and I hope you have a little better idea at this point of why you are a Southern Baptist, if you are, and more importantly, why you are a Christian. You are now at a point where you are going to make a decision. It may be a very positive decision to follow Christ in all of His teachings. Or it may be a subconscious decision to just go with the flow and not get too involved. I sincerely hope it is the former. There is nothing more disappointing than to see people give their lives to Christ and then within days or weeks fall right back into the same old mode of living for themselves.

Do you remember the scripture we read in 2 Corinthians at the end of the last chapter? Go back for a moment to 2 Corinthians 9:12. It is not only our money that should be dedicated to God, but also our time and talents. The service we perform for God is just as important as giving our money. You may feel very inadequate as a new Christian as to what helpful service you could perform for God. Read Matthew 25:31-46 and Ephesians 5:1-11. What do those verses say to you? These passages of Scripture show me a number of little things that we can do that will be pleasing to God. We talked earlier about glorifying God in what we do. These are the things that glorify Him.

When you see a place where you can minister in God's name, and you feel God is already at work there, just jump in and do it. You don't need to be invited or begged. Just be sure God is in it. The New Beginning has to start with your personal life. It is vital for you to start immediately, if you are not already doing so, to study your Bible and pray *every day.* Arrange your schedule now to free up fifteen minutes at a time each day where you can put everything else aside and read God's Word and pray to Him. This is vital to your Christian growth. Look at I Corinthians 3:1-3. Don't let your spiritual growth be stunted by not studying and praying each day. We talked about this earlier, but it needs repeated emphasis because some Christians never get beyond the "milk" stage in their spiritual growth and never mature in their walk with God.

Let me mention a few places where you can put your talents to work for Him. Open your Bible to 1 Peter 4:8-11. Certainly, all of us have the ability to love and to show concern for someone who is hurting. We can help someone in need. We can pray for those in our church family who are going through problems. Many churches provide a list of those who have special needs. Some churches have a prayer room where we can volunteer to spend a little time once a week to pray for our church family, for missionaries, and for other needs made known to our church.

Ask whoever leads the youth in your church if there is a young person in your church who needs help. If you are good at math or reading or science or any other subject, you may be able to tutor one of the young people who is having problems at school in that subject. Or you may have someone in your church that is struggling with English. You could help them learn how to read or write. One-on-one tutoring is a tremendous blessing to the one being helped. It will make you a friend for life. After you have grown as a Christian, you may want to offer to be a mentor for new Christians in your church.

I recently read of a missionary in Niger who teaches men and women to sew to enable them to make a living. You may be a good seamstress or carpenter or auto mechanic or cook. I will almost guarantee you there is someone in your church, or a non-Christian who lives near you that would be thrilled for you to share your expertise with them. It's that old story of "Give a man a fish and he will eat for a day. Teach him how to fish and he will eat for the rest of his life."

There are groups of people in almost all of our churches who offer their services to help build or repair churches or other buildings. I am the world's worst carpenter, but I spent some very worthwhile Saturdays working with a building team repairing churches damaged in a hurricane. The people in charge gave me a wrecking bar and I tore out the old, damaged walls so they could be replaced. I proved you don't have to be skilled to contribute.

Four hundred men and women from Texas churches spent a summer building a new building for the Canadian Southern Baptist Seminary, a building that could not have been built for several years if the seminary had to pay for the labor.

I have several friends involved in prison ministry. Most of them teach *Experiencing God* to the prison inmates, with some unbelievable results. Many of the prisoners are becoming Christians and are avid Bible students. In some states there are prison ministries in almost every prison. Prison ministries around the country are changing the lives of many inmates and reducing the number of those who return to prison. Your pastor or associational missionary will know the names of those involved in this kind of ministry in your area.

This will also work in the county jail. If there isn't a ministry of this type in your area, contact your state convention office and see if training is available to enable you to start such a ministry.

How about teaching Sunday school? "Who, me?" you ask. "I am a new Christian, I don't have the ability or knowledge to teach." Let me say first of all that you will always learn more by teaching than by sitting in a class. So start preparing to teach. When your church or association offers training for teachers, attend, even if you are not yet teaching. Learn all you can learn.

This goes back to our previous discussions about Bible study. If you only open your Bible on Sunday morning, you will never learn enough to teach. If you take advantage of the opportunities to learn, you will find very quickly that you will grasp enough fundamentals to start teaching. Bible dictionaries, concordances, study books, commentaries, and other helps are all available in your church library, if you have one, or at a local Christian bookstore. A Lifeway bookstore in a large city near you is an excellent place to look.

You can approach teaching in several different ways. You can volunteer to fill in for your teacher when he is going to be away on a Sunday. Have him let you know in advance, and perhaps he will even help you plan an outline before he leaves. Or start in the young children's departments where helpers are always needed. Ask if you can teach the Bible story. Teaching is very rewarding and will assist you in the learning process if you will get involved.

Sign up for the training courses in your church. *Experiencing God, Master Life,* and many other excellent courses are offered in most churches. If they aren't offered, ask your minister of education or pastor to get the books for you. You might even ask if there are others who would like to join you in the study.

If you want to know more about how your church operates, get on a committee. Find out who the chairman of the committee on committees is and volunteer your services. If you are a young person, you may want to serve on the youth committee. If you are a businessman or woman, ask to serve on the budget or finance committees. If you have manual skills such as carpentry or plumbing, you may want to be on the building maintenance committee.

Just asking to be on a committee doesn't guarantee that you will be asked to serve, but it is a good starting point. I have heard people complain, "I have been in this church twenty years and have never been asked to serve on a committee." My first question is, "Have you ever told anyone you wanted to be on a committee?" The answer is almost always, "No." Those who are responsible for filling committee rosters are always anxious to get the job done with the best people, but oftentimes they don't know everyone in the church, or what their talents are. Let them know that you want to serve. If you don't get asked the first year, be persistent and remember that the committee on committees chairperson will change almost every year, so keep the new chairperson up to date with your request.

Volunteer! I have never been in a church where there was not an almost continuous need for volunteers. The choir is putting on a pageant or program, and there are chairs to be moved, scenery to be built, costumes to be sewn. Don't volunteer to do more than you can comfortably do, but pick out something you can do and do it well.

A big church dinner is being planned. Tables need to be set up, food prepared, invitations sent out, promotional material prepared, the floor needs mopping. Pick a job, and volunteer to do it. Show everyone you can do it right, and don't worry about being asked again. You will be a popular person in your church.

Your church music program is an excellent place to serve and to make friends. Join the choir. If you can't sing, offer to help with the children's choir program. Just keeping order is a big help to the teacher. Your church may have an orchestra or a worship team. If you play an instrument, you can almost always find places to use your talents. Piano players in particular are always in great demand. You may have an opportunity to play hymns for one Sunday school department and then go to your own department for Bible study. Let your minister of music know that you play an instrument. There can also be opportunities to play for services in nearby nursing homes or retirement centers.

Inquire to see if your church may be sponsoring a mission church in the ghetto or with a minority group. You don't have to speak the language to help. It doesn't take a second language to wield a paint brush or a hammer to help fix up the mission building. If you speak the language, so much the better. Volunteer to teach English to the kids or run a recreation program.

Vacation Bible School is an excellent place to get involved. Every summer, most churches have a VBS program for the kids. There are never enough helpers. If your time schedule permits, offer to help. If your days are tied up with a job, you might ask if your church has an evening program in the summer for the teenagers. They can almost always use help.

You may also check to see if some of the smaller churches in your community could use some help with a summer program. You might even offer to go out of town to help a small church in a rural community.

This brings me to volunteer missions. We touched on it lightly before. The programs that took me to Tanzania and my wife and me to Canada were volunteer mission programs. The International Mission Board and the North American Mission Board, as well as your state convention and your association, all get involved in volunteer programs that call for as little as one or two days or as much as two years. The Mission Service Corps is one such program. No matter what your skills, you will amazed at the opportunities. Building teams, administrators, health care professionals, teaching, agricultural skills, and many more talents are always needed, many for limited times. If you can afford to pay your own way, so much the better, but if you have the skills and desire without the funds, let your pastor know. There may be someone else in your church who has the money. These are not vacation trips. Go, expecting to work hard.

There may come a point in your life when you feel God calling you to full-time Christian service. This may mean some radical changes in your life, but don't neglect God's call. Every missionary, preacher, minister of music, education minister, and youth minister no doubt had other plans at one point in his or her life. Don't think you "feel the call" to be a full-time Christian worker because it looks easy or because it looks like a good way to make a living. It is very hard and difficult work, and you will last only if God has called you to it. If you feel led in this direction, I would suggest you talk with your pastor and then to the president or vice president of the seminary nearest you. They are good listeners and good advisors. They can help you discern whether you really have been chosen by God for full-time Christian work. Actually, we have all been chosen for full-time duty, which brings me to my last point.

I saved this until last for a reason. I honestly believe every Christian should be a volunteer in God's army to share the Gospel with others. There is not one person who will read this book who doesn't know someone who is lost. It may be a relative, a friend, a neighbor or a working acquaintance, maybe even a fellow student. That person is going to go to hell unless someone does something about it. Jesus Christ did something about it. He died on the cross for that individual. That was the hard part. Your responsibility is to share the Good News with that person. Matthew 28:16-20 tells us what Jesus thought was important. It was His last instruction to His disciples before He ascended back into heaven.

There is no valid excuse for not sharing. If you won the Publisher Clearing House Sweepstakes, you would shout it all over town and print it in your Christmas newsletter. The news you have to share about Jesus is far greater in value. Don't let someone you know suffer in Hell for eternity because you were too timid or bashful to share with them.

If you don't feel capable, ask your pastor or Sunday School teacher to go with you, but learn how to witness about the Good News early on, and then share every time you get the chance.

There are several ways to do this. I use a booklet I mentioned earlier, called the Four Spiritual Laws. You can buy it in a Christian bookstore if your church doesn't have a supply. All you have to do is to be able to read. It even has the prayer for them to accept God printed out.

You may want to mark your Bible with the Roman Road scriptures. These are all scriptures in the book of Romans that will lead your friends to Christ. Your pastor or a deacon in your church can show you how.

Start sharing now. You will not always get a warm reception. Some will say no. But your job is to witness. God does the convicting, and it may be several years after you plant the seed before they will accept Him.

I promise you this. The day you lead someone else to Christ will be the greatest day in your life, as well as his or hers. I pray faithfully that God will cross my path with someone I can witness to, and I could write another chapter on some of the great times I have had in sharing God's Word. If you really want to see the Holy Spirit at work, start the practice of praying that you will have an opportunity to witness. Then follow through.

God gave His grace to make us whole,
So we can fill a different role.
He wants our life to count for more,
To lead our friends to His open door.

He wants us to praise and to glorify
His risen Son who lives on high;
To change our ways, to live for Him,
Living lives that are free from sin.

To be an example, pure and right,
A glowing lamp, to shed His light.
This is His charge to you and me,
And why He died to set us free.

We give our lives, or so we say,
But put off change 'til another day.
"We'll do it tomorrow, maybe next week.
Yes, we love Him—It's His way we seek."

Why do Christians not always obey?
Are we truly seeking to follow God's way?
If we love Him as much as we say we do,
Why not live a life that is pure and true?

Let's be an example that others can see—
Christ Jesus, only, living in me.
Others will follow if we show the way,
Not some time later, but starting today.

A New Beginning is what we need,
A change in our lifestyle, in word and in deed.
Let's please our Savior, live for Him this day;
Start by reading His Word, and bowing to pray.

May God bless you in this New Beginning.

Daily Study Material

Please do these lessons daily. Do not do all of one week's lessons at one sitting. I hope to encourage you to get in the habit of studying your Bible and praying each day, and to continue this habit long after you have finished studying this book. Try to set aside the same time each day to read the material, answer the questions, and pray.

Read the chapter on Monday or spread it out through the week, whichever works best for you. Then each day do the required study material. In chapter 11 you will be asked to contact some resource people to gather information. You may want to preview that week's lessons so you can prepare in advance.

Be sure to look up all Bible references as you read. They are the foundational part of your study program. It will also give you good practice in locating scriptures in your Bible.

CHAPTER ONE
AM I REALLY SAVED?

WEEKLY MEMORY VERSE: John 3:16

MONDAY: *READ:* John 3:16; Romans 3:23; Romans 5:8; Ephesians 2:8-9

MEMORIZE: Four Spiritual Laws:

LAW ONE: God loves you and offers a wonderful plan for your life.

LAW TWO: Man is sinful and separated from God. Therefore he cannot know and experience God's love and plan for his life.

LAW THREE: Jesus Christ is God's only provision for man's sin. Through Him you can know and experience God's love and plan for your life.

LAW FOUR: We must individually receive Jesus Christ as Savior and Lord; then we can know and experience God's love and plan for our lives.

PRAY: That God will help you memorize these four laws.

TUESDAY: *READ:* Matthew 26:69-75; Acts 2
ANSWER: How did Peter change from the Matthew scripture to the Acts scripture?

PRAY: That you will speak out boldly for Christ.

WEDNESDAY: READ: Acts 24:13-27
ANSWER: Why did Paul's life change?

PRAY: That Christ's resurrection will be real to you.

THURSDAY: *READ:* Acts 7:58; Acts 8:1-3; Acts 9:1-31
ANSWER: How did Paul's life change?

What was the reason for his change?

PRAY: That you will be as zealous as Paul in telling the Good News.

FRIDAY: *READ:* Acts. 2:21; John 5:24; Philippians 3:20-21
ANSWER: Our promise of Salvation is contingent on

_____ & _____ .

What does it mean to repent?

PRAY: God will make you aware of your sins and help you to break any bad habits.

CHAPTER TWO
WHO THE HOLY SPIRIT IS AND WHAT HE DOES

WEEKLY MEMORY VERSE: 2 TIMOTHY 3:16

MONDAY: THE HOLY SPIRIT IN CREATION
READ: Psalm 104:30, and Job 33:4
ANSWER: What does Elihu tell Job?

PRAY: Thank God for creating you, your parents, and your grandparents.

TUESDAY: THE HOLY SPIRIT AT WORK
READ: Numbers 27:18; Daniel 5:11-14; Exodus 31:1-5; Judges 14:6
ANSWER: What did Joshua, Daniel, Bezalel, and Samson have in common?

PRAY: Ask God to help you turn over control of your life to the Holy Spirit.

WEDNESDAY: HOW THE HOLY SPIRIT DOES GOD'S WORK
READ: 2 Timothy 3:16; John 16:7-11; John 14:16

ANSWER: What did Jesus promise about the Counselor (Holy Spirit)?

PRAY: That the Holy Spirit will guide you in all things.

THURSDAY: THE GIFT OF THE SPIRIT
READ: Acts 2:38; Ephesians 1:13-14; John 16:12-15
ANSWER: What does the Spirit guarantee?

PRAY: Thank God for the gift of the Holy Spirit.

FRIDAY: HOW THE HOLY SPIRIT HELPS US
READ: Romans 8:14-16; Romans 8:26-39
ANSWER: How does the Holy Spirit help us?

PRAY: That the Holy Spirit will help you to know what to pray for.

CHAPTER THREE
THE HOLY BIBLE

WEEKLY MEMORY VERSE: MEMORIZE NAMES OF BOOKS OF OLD TESTAMENT

MONDAY: Memorize the names of the first tens book of the Bible.
PRAY: God will help you to learn the names of all the books of the Old Testament this week.

TUESDAY: Memorize the names of the next ten books of the Bible and then practice saying the first twenty in the order they appear.
PRAY: God will guide you in the purchase of your Bible and in its daily use.

WEDNESDAY: Memorize the names of the next ten books of the Old Testament and then practice saying the first thirty in sequence.

    PRAY: That you will become familiar with how to find things in your Bible.

THURSDAY: Memorize the last nine names of the books of the Old Testament and practice saying all thirty-nine in proper order.

    PRAY: That God will help you to stay faithful in studying His Word each day.

FRIDAY: Practice saying the names of all the Old Testament books in their proper sequence. Stay with it until you can say them to someone else.

    PRAY: Commit to God that you will read the Bible through in twelve months as soon as you complete this course.

CHAPTER FOUR
WHY DO I NEED TO GO TO CHURCH?

WEEKLY MEMORY VERSE: HEBREWS 10:25

MONDAY: *READ:* Hebrews 10:21-25; Joshua 22:27
    ANSWER: What habit are we encouraged to pursue?

    PRAY: Thank God for your church and its staff.

TUESDAY: *READ:* Psalm 95:6; Psalm 100:2; Matthew 4:10
    ANSWER: What do these verses command us to do?

    PRAY: That you will be faithful in your worship of God.

WEDNESDAY: *READ:* John 4:24; Acts 2:41-44
    ANSWER: What did the early Christians devote themselves to?

PRAY: That your worship will be worthy.

THURSDAY: *READ:* 1 Corinthians 12
ANSWER: What happens if I fail to use my God-given gifts to do my part at church?

PRAY: That God will help you to discover your gifts.

FRIDAY: *READ:* 1 Thessalonians 1:1-10
ANSWER: What were some of the attributes of the church at Thessalonica?

PRAY: That your church will glorify God in all that it does.

CHAPTER FIVE
REPENTANCE

WEEKLY MEMORY VERSE: ROMANS 3:23-24

MONDAY: *READ:* Romans 3:23 and Romans 6:1-14.
ANSWER: Who is included in 3:23?

Does that mean you?

PRAY: That this week each of us will be aware of our own sins.

TUESDAY: *READ:* Acts 20:21; Acts 2:38; Matthew 4:17; Mark 6:12 and Luke 13:3.
ANSWER: Is repentance an option or a mandate?

PRAY: That God will make clear to you any unconfessed sin in your life.

WEDNESDAY: *READ:* Romans 2:1-13.
   ANSWER: Are we opening ourselves up to God's judgment when we ignore the sin in our lives?

   PRAY: That God will forgive you for all of your sins and help you to start on the road to repentance.

THURSDAY: *READ:* 1 Corinthians 6:19 and 2 Chronicles 29:15-19.
   ANSWER: What needs to be done to purify your temple, where the Holy Spirit resides?

   PRAY: That God will help you to purify yourself and keep yourself pure so the Holy Spirit will reside in a pure, clean temple.

FRIDAY: *READ:* 2 Samuel 12:1-19 and Psalm 32:3-4.
   ANSWER: Was one night of pleasure worth the agony? How many other lives are affected when we sin?

   PRAY: That repentance will mean more to you than just saying you're sorry; that your life will show the fruit of repentance.

CHAPTER SIX
WHAT IS EXPECTED OF ME AS A CHRISTIAN?

WEEKLY MEMORY VERSE: MARK 12:30-31

MONDAY: *READ:* Exodus 20:1-17
   ANSWER: Name three changes you could expect to see if our world obeyed the Ten Commandments.

   PRAY: That God will make you aware of any of the commandments you are not keeping and help you to change.

TUESDAY: *READ:* Matthew 5, 6, 7
   ANSWER: Name one attribute from each chapter you would like to develop.

   PRAY: That God will help you develop these attributes.

WEDNESDAY: *READ:* Mark 12:28-31
   ANSWER: What message do you get from this passage?

Who is first in your life?

Romans 5:6-8. Is God's love for everyone?

1 John 3:17-18. How do you show God's love?

PRAY: For one person you need to learn to love.

THURSDAY: *READ:* 1 Corinthians 6:12-19
   ANSWER: Name one habit you would like to break.

 2 Thessalonians 2:13 How will God help you to accomplish breaking that habit?

PRAY: God will assist you in breaking that bad habit.

FRIDAY: *READ:* 2 Timothy 2:15
   ANSWER: Why is it important to study God's word?

PRAY: God will show you a time each day when you can faithfully pray and study His Word.

CHAPTER SEVEN
MAKE IT A MATTER OF PRAYER

WEEKLY MEMORY VERSE: 1 THESSALONIANS 5:16

MONDAY:

ANSWER: Who and what did you pray for today? If you have not prayed today, do so now and then make your list. Buy a small notebook and start a prayer journal. Make a list by date of what you pray for and then mark the date the prayer is answered and how it is answered.

PRAY: That you will learn to pray for persons outside your family circle.

TUESDAY:

Look up the word Prayer in the concordance of your Bible and then read at least five of the Scriptures listed. Write down the ones you read and who or what was prayed for.

PRAY: For someone in your church who is ill or in need.

WEDNESDAY: *READ:* MATTHEW 6:5-15

ANSWER: What do we call this prayer?

Outline Jesus' prayer. You should be able to list at least three things he included in His prayer.

PRAY: For something you thought about while studying the Lord's Prayer.

THURSDAY: *READ:* James 4:8

ANSWER: How can you draw near to God?

Psalm 86. What impresses you as being important here?

(READ TOMORROW'S ASSIGNMENT NOW)

FRIDAY: Before you do anything else Friday morning,
   READ: 1 Thessalonians 5:17; James 5:15-16; 2 Chronicles 7:14
   ANSWER: Look for situations all day where a word of prayer could be uttered for someone, and then pray. Make notes of who and what you pray for. Bring the list with you on Sunday. You will not turn it in. No one else will see it.

CHAPTER EIGHT
WHY DO CHRISTIANS SOMETIMES SUFFER?

WEEKLY MEMORY VERSE: JOB 42:5-6

MONDAY: *READ:*Genesis 4:3-14; Genesis 37:14-28; Genesis 39:10-20
   ANSWER: Who suffered in these situations?

Did they cause their own problems?

PRAY: For someone you know who is suffering.

TUESDAY: List any things that you do could bring harm or suffering to you. Think about eating, drinking, gambling, driving habits, or any other risks you take.
   Pray: God will help you break a specific habit you want to be rid of.

READ: Job 38:1-12
   ANSWER: Can man begin to understand how great God is?

WEDNESDAY: *READ:* Job 42:1-6
   Why did Job repent?

PRAY: Thank God for His creation of the world.

THURSDAY: *READ:* Romans 8:26-39
    ANSWER: In verse 28, what are the conditions for everything working together for good?

In verse 32, did God ever suffer?

PRAY: Thank God that He was willing for Jesus to suffer on the cross for you.

FRIDAY: *READ:* Daniel 3
    ANSWER: Why were Shadrach, Meshach, and Abednego thrown in the furnace?

Why were they saved from a fiery death? (v. 28)

PRAY: Thank God that He is with us when we suffer.

CHAPTER NINE
BAPTISM AND THE LORD'S SUPPER

WEEKLY MEMORY VERSE: 1 CORINTHIANS 11:26

MONDAY: *READ:* Luke 3:2-22; John 3:16-18; Acts 16:30-31
    ANSWER: What did John urge the crowd to do? (v. 8)

PRAY: That God will make you aware of anything you need to repent of.

TUESDAY: *READ:* Luke 13:2-8; Acts 16:30-31
    ANSWER: What two things are necessary for salvation?

_____ and _____ .

After you meet the above requirements, what should follow? (Acts 16:33)

PRAY: Thank God He made salvation possible for us.

WEDNESDAY: *READ:* Matthew 28:19-20
ANSWER: Name three things Jesus commanded.

Be sure to practice saying the names of the Old Testament books.
PRAY: Ask God to give you the courage to share His love with someone else.

THURSDAY: *READ:* Exodus 12:1-36; Mark 14:1-16
ANSWER: What did Passover signify?

PRAY: That you will always prepare your heart and mind for the Lord's Supper.

FRIDAY: *READ:* Mark 14:17-24; 1Corinthians 11:23-29
ANSWER: What does the bread and fruit of the vine represent?

PRAY: Thank God for the sacrifice of Jesus on the cross.

CHAPTER TEN
SOUTHERN BAPTISTS—WHO ARE THEY?

WEEKLY MEMORY VERSE: NAMES OF BOOKS IN NEW TESTAMENT

MONDAY: *READ:* Acts 8:26-40; Matthew 28:19-20; Acts 11:19-26
ANSWER: Did Philip follow Jesus' command?

PRAY: That we will be as faithful in obeying Jesus as Philip was.

TUESDAY: Memorize the names of the first ten books of the New Testament.
PRAY: Thank God for those men and women down through the years who have been faithful to God's commands.

WEDNESDAY: Memorize the names of next ten New Testament books.
PRAY: Thank God for early Baptists in Europe who were true to God's Word.

THURSDAY: Memorize the names of the last nine books in the New Testament.
PRAY: Thank God for the early Southern Baptists in the United States who made great sacrifice to build the first Southern Baptist churches.

FRIDAY: Practice saying all the books of the Bible in sequence. Do this each day until you are comfortable saying them by memory.
PRAY: Thank God for present-day Southern Baptist leaders and ask God to help us to stay true to His Word.

CHAPTER ELEVEN
HOW SOUTHERN BAPTISTS ARE ORGANIZED

WEEKLY MEMORY VERSE: 1 TIMOTHY 3:13

MONDAY: *READ:* 1Timothy 3:1-6; 1Timothy 5:17-20; Titus 1:5-2:8
ANSWER: Name three qualifications of a pastor (overseer).

Name three duties of a pastor.

PRAY: For your pastor, that he will be kept strong in the faith.

TUESDAY: Ask your Sunday school teacher for a list of all the staff members in your church. Learn their names and what they are responsible for.
PRAY: For all the staff members in your church.

WEDNESDAY: *READ:* 1 Timothy 1:8-13
ANSWER: Name three qualifications of a deacon.

PRAY: Thank God for your pastor, the church, staff, and the deacons.

THURSDAY: Ask your church secretary for a list of the deacons in your church.
PRAY: For each deacon in your church.

FRIDAY: With the aid of your mentor, a deacon, or someone in the church office, compile a list of names of your association missionary, his associate, the state executive director, and the editor of your state paper.
PRAY: For all of the above.

CHAPTER TWELVE
WHERE THE MONEY COMES FROM

WEEKLY MEMORY VERSE: JOHN 1:3

MONDAY: *READ:* 2 Corinthians 1:21-22; John 1:3
   ANSWER: Who created all things and owns all things?

PRAY: Thank God for all of His blessings. See how many things you can name that you are thankful for without asking for anything.

TUESDAY: *READ:* Romans 8:12-21; 1 Corinthians 2:14
   ANSWER: What is our inheritance?

PRAY: Thank God that you are one of His children and a "joint heir" with Jesus Christ.

WEDNESDAY: *READ:* Leviticus 27:30; Malachi 3:8-12
   ANSWER: Did God expect His people to return a portion of what He had given them?

Why should we give to Him?

PRAY: That you will be faithful in giving back to God a portion of what He has given to you.

THURSDAY: *READ:* Romans 12:1-2; Ephesians 5:15
   ANSWER: What are our responsibilities to God?

PRAY: That God will help you to be a responsible person.

FRIDAY: *READ:* 2 Corinthians 9:6-15
   ANSWER: This was Paul's encouragement to the church at Corinth to be generous in sharing with the Jerusalem church that was having financial difficulty. Is there a lesson here for us?
What is it?

PRAY: That we will learn to be generous with what God has blessed us with.

CHAPTER THIRTEEN
IT'S UP TO YOU!

WEEKLY MEMORY VERSE: MATTHEW 28:19

MONDAY: *READ:* Matthew 25:31-46; Ephesians 51-11
ANSWER: What is our responsibility?

PRAY: That God will help you meet your responsibility.

TUESDAY: *READ:* 1 Peter 4:8-11
ANSWER: Name three things this scripture says we need to be doing.

PRAY: That you can live up to these commands.

WEDNESDAY: Review the names of all the books of the Bible. You should be able to name them all by memory. *PRAY:* Thank God for your mentor, teacher, or whoever helped you through this course. Commit to helping a new Christian go through the course in the near future.

THURSDAY: *READ:* Matthew 28:16-20
ANSWER: What did Jesus instruct us to do?

REVIEW THE FOUR SPIRITUAL LAWS
PRAY: That God will help you to learn how to use the Four Spiritual Laws booklet.

FRIDAY: Make a list of at least three people you know who don't know Jesus. Commit to sharing the Four Spiritual Laws with them.

PRAY: That God will use the Holy Spirit to open the minds of those you have listed and give you the wisdom to share God's love with them.

Bibliography

Armstrong, O.K. & Marjorie, *The Indomitable Baptists,* Doubleday (1967)

Baxter, J. Sidlow, *Explore the Book,* Zondervan (1964)

Dilmore, Don, *The First One Hundred Years,* Eakin (1988)

Dobson, James, *When God Doesn't Make Sense,* Tyndale (1993)

Hallock, E. F., *Always in Prayer,* Broadman, (1966)

Hobbs, Herschel H., *The Baptist Faith & Message,* Convention Press, (1971)

Swindoll, Charles, *The Bride,* Zondervan (1994)

Swindoll, Charles, *David,* Word Books, (1997)

Vedder, Henry C., *A Short History of the Baptists,* Judson Press, (1907)

Wiersbe, Warren, *Why Us?,* Revell, (1984)

For Further Reading

All of the books listed in the bibliography.

Grace Awakening, Charles Swindoll, (Word).

Flying Closer to the Flame, Charles Swindoll, (Word).

In His Steps, Charles Sheldon, (Broadman).

Flowers and Fruits in the Wilderness, Z.N. Morell, (Baylor Press).

Master Your Money, Ron Blue, (Nelson).

Obedience–The Key to Prosperity, Wayne Coleman, (Cross Reference).

My Utmost for His Highest, Oswald Chambers, (Barbour)

Commission & OnMission magazines published by the International and North American Mission Boards.

Training Courses

Experiencing God, Blackaby & King, (Lifeway)

Master Life, Willis, (Lifeway).

Order Form

Postal orders:
Don Dilmore, 21 Edgewood CT., Montgomery, TX. 77356

Telephone orders: (409) 449-4998

Please send *New Beginnings* to:

Name: _____

Address: _____

City: _____ State: _____

Zip: _____

Telephone: (____) _____

Book Price: $10.00 in U.S. dollars.

Sales Tax: Please add 6.25% for books shipped to an Texas address.

Shipping: $2.00 for the first book and $1.00 for each additional book to cover shipping and handling within US, Canada, and Mexico. International orders add $4.00 for the first book and $2.00 for each additional book.

Quantity Discounts Available - Please call for information
(409) 449-4998